For the Doyles —
God bless 'em
Sr. M. Agatha

THE HISTORY OF HOUSTON HEIGHTS

From Its Foundation in 1891
To Its Annexation in 1918
by
Sister M. Agatha

OSCAR MARTIN CARTER, Founder of Houston Heights

THE HISTORY OF

HOUSTON
HEIGHTS

1891 - 1918

By

SISTER M. AGATHA
INCARNATE WORD ACADEMY
HOUSTON, TEXAS

Illustrated by

VICTOR J. GREEN

PREMIER PRINTING COMPANY
HOUSTON, TEXAS
1956

Library of Congress Catalog Card Number 56-12249

Dedicated to my parents
Michael and Frieda Sheehan
In gratitude for a happy childhood
spent in the
HEIGHTS

FOREWORD

This modest little book makes no pretense of being a definitive history of the Heights. Nor does it speak with authority as free from error. Of necessity much material was collected from early settlers by way of reminiscences; and even though conclusions were reached by corroborating testimony of many persons, still without positive proof, in some instances erroneous statements might be presented as facts.

This work is intended to be a stimulus to further research. Its only excuse for being is that a modest beginning is better than no start.

Now a word about *who* is in the book. The table of contents shows the outline as designed to give a general picture of the early days in Houston Heights before annexation in 1918. Names fell into place when they were connected in the record with the subject under consideration. However, it could easily happen that with so little recorded data for foundation work in this history, a primary fact might be omitted and an important name pass unnoticed. In all charity please believe that an honest effort has been made to avoid such occurrences.

WHO HELPED
TO WRITE THIS HISTORY

This work was an accident. I merely intended making a scrapbook for the Heights Library and had promised Miss Jimmie May Hicks, the Librarian, to correct (as far as I was able) newspaper clippings in the scrapbook. Then the correction notes began going deeper and my own notes began getting thicker. At that time Miss Hicks and I decided to keep my own notes intact and separate from the scrapbook. To Miss Hicks then, to her assistant, Mrs. Elizabeth Hinckley, and to the other members of the staff of the Heights Library goes first acknowledgment of help received.

Next, Mr. and Mrs. Arthur W. Cooley and Mr. and Mrs. P. V. Myers made available their pictures and clippings and gave liberally of their fund of information on the early days.

We advertised in the newspaper for help and Miss Nellie Kennedy and C. V. Kroning came forward with concrete facts. Mrs. Lottie Peacock's assistance, too, was invaluable.

Judge W. G. Love, first mayor of the Heights, has no living descendant; but Miss Helen Milroy, daughter of the second mayor, cooperated most generously. Mayor D. Barker is still living, and he and his daughter, Mrs. J. F. Gale, aided the work. The widow of Mayor R. F. Isbell, Mrs. Ruby Isbell, gave freely from her papers and from her accurate memory for details. Mayor Marmion's son, J. B. Marmion, Jr., furnished enough clippings and pictures to make a separate scrapbook of his father's term of office. He also assisted in getting other material from old residents.

Mrs. Charles Lucas gave us a view-book of the Heights. These old books were put out by O. M. Carter's office and once were to be found in every home in the Heights, but few people saved them. Today they are rare and valuable. Mrs.

8

Anna Marie Durham, widow of Fire Chief J. L. Durham, sent notes on the early fire department; and Horace Olive, grandson of Dr. William Olive, gave us other material on the volunteer fire department. Many other residents also sent pictures or clippings, maps, and copies of papers.

But in this outline of history, quite apart from the collection for the scrapbooks and for the files at the library, each of the following persons aided in a definite way with either specific information or help in obtaining data.

Mrs. Harriet Dickson Reynolds, Librarian for the City of Houston, procured for us the file of the *Suburbanite*. At the Main Library, the staff in the Texas Room on the third floor and the reference department of the second floor extended every aid and courtesy.

Andrew Forest Muir, historian, and Miss Ruby Bernard, in the Office of the County Clerk, Harris County (both residents of the Heights) helped with information on deed records. Edwin A. Bonewitz (also a resident of the Heights) gave generously of his accumulation of notes and material and aided in obtaining help beyond his own files.

Tony Triolo, of the *Houston Press,* assisted with photography work. R. J. Watts extended courtesies asked of the *Houston Chronicle*. George Fuermann of the *Houston Post* read the first pages and gave encouragement.

Mrs. O. F. Carroll and Mrs. Bess Whitehead Scott read the manuscript and made valuable suggestions. Arthur Lefevre, Jr. rendered editorial assistance. Mrs. Thomas Taylor of the Rein Company answered every call for help. Mrs. J. F. Boyle and Miss Mary Catherine Boyle ran down all sources of information and stood ready to help with any errand.

To the Sisters of my religious community, who were generous and understanding in helping me in a dozen different ways, and to my old pupils, who drove me about while collecting material, I am grateful.

For the errors that may have crept into the account I alone am responsible.

TABLE OF CONTENTS

CHAPTER I

THE DEVELOPMENT OF A SUBURBAN ADDITION

CHAPTER II

THE GOVERNMENT

CHAPTER III
PROFESSIONAL LIFE

CHAPTER IV
SOCIAL LIFE

CHAPTER V
CLUBS, SOCIAL SERVICE ORGANIZATIONS, LODGES

CHAPTER VI
BIOGRAPHY

LIST OF ILLUSTRATIONS

THE DEVELOPMENT
OF A
SUBURBAN ADDITION

OMAHA & SOUTH TEXAS LAND CO.

OFFICES:
208 MAIN STREET, HOUSTON,
AND
HOUSTON HEGHTS,

O. M. CARTER, PRES.
CARROLL M. CARTER, VICE PRES.
JOHN A. MILROY, SEC'Y.
D. D. COOLEY, TREAS.
C. S. MONTGOMERY.
W. J. CONNERY.

HOUSTON, TEXAS,

THE OMAHA AND SOUTH TEXAS LAND COMPANY

The Omaha and South Texas Land Company was organized in Nebraska about 1887 and derived its name from the fact that Nebraska interests bought some 1,765 acres of land northwest of Houston, Texas. Oscar Martin Carter of Omaha was President of the First National Bank of Ashland, Nebraska, and Daniel Denton Cooley was cashier. It was Mr. Carter who bought the Texas land; but as president of the new land company, he necessarily spent much time in the North and in the East, so that he sent Mr. Cooley to reside in Houston as representative and trustee to direct active development of the huge tract. The *Houston Daily Herald* in 1893 published an impressive pamphlet titled *Houston Illustrated, a Few Facts* . . . which gives a lengthy account of the development of the Heights and mentions that "Mr. D. D. Cooley, the treasurer of the company, is in charge of affairs . . ." and then. "N. L. Mills is Superintendent of the Real Estate Department."

In the *City Directory, 1892-1893* an advertisement names the directors of the Omaha and South Texas Land Company for that year:

O. M. Carter, Omaha, Neb., President
C. S. Montgomery, Omaha, Neb., Vice-President
Philip Potter, Omaha, Neb., Sec'y
D. D. Cooley, Treasurer and General Manager

And on the opposite side of the advertisement are more directors:

D. D. Cooley, Houston, Texas
W. J. Connery, Boston, Mass.
F. E. Clarke, Lawrence, Mass.
G. B. Hengen, Engineer in charge

BRASHEAR'S JOHN AUSTIN GRANT

The land from which Houston Heights was carved was originally known as Brashear's John Austin Grant, or the upper league part of the two-league grant.

John Austin had obtained the two leagues from the Mexican government in 1824. He died of cholera in 1833, and his wife inherited the land.* The following year, after her marriage to T. F. L. Parrott, she settled the estate by ceding to John Austin's father the upper or western league. But the father died of cholera in 1834, and his portion then went to his next son and heir, William T. Austin.

In 1836, the Allen Brothers enter the picture, seeking to buy land for their proposed town of Houston. Elizabeth E. Parrott and her husband then sold the lower league and William T. Austin likewise disposed of his upper league, both to A. C. and J. K. Allen.

By 1838 the Allens had paid the remainder of their $5,000 obligation to the Parrotts and the town of Houston was a reality. However, in 1839, the Allens ran into financial difficulties. They were forced by sheriff's order (for debt) to sell 600 acres (at approximately $1.00 an acre) of the upper league to Thomas William Ward. Gradually the whole of the upper league slipped from joint ownership with the lower league that had become Houston.

In 1891, when Carter's agents were negotiating, most of the tract originally known as the upper league was owned

*It has been erroneously stated in one text that John Austin's wife and two children died in the same epidemic. Whether or not the children died, it is certain that the wife lived and later married T.F.L. Parrott.

by Mrs. Sarah Brashear, widow of I. W. Brashear, who had acquired the land in 1872. The Allens had paid $1.00 an acre in 1836; Carter's company paid $45 an acre a little over fifty years later.

The tract was 75 feet above sea level and 23 feet above the level of downtown Houston. The name Houston Heights then was a natural title and gave confidence to people hunting a healthful location. It is a matter of history that during the terrible yellow fever epidemics that periodically struck Houston, many people fled to the Heights and camped out until the siege subsided. The West Montgomery Road that ran through the woods was well traveled.

The sale of lots in the Heights did not begin until 1892. A few of the early residents recall that the panic of 1893 hurt development and made some prospective buyers fearful about the purchase of real estate at that time. However, there are too many pamphlets and view books printed around 1893 and 1894, with actual photographs of industries and concrete evidence of real estate development, to permit any doubt about the almost stupendous beginning of the Heights.

Other associates had joined Mr. Carter and Mr. Cooley. C. A. McKinney, N. L. Mills, and John A. Milroy linked their names with the first two members of the land company to make up what might be called "the first five citizens" directly responsible for the development of the Heights. Only Mr. Mills of the group seems early to have severed direct connection with the Heights when he left to resume his real estate business in Houston. However, his short stay was commemorated with music in his honor. Clifford Grunewald composed *"Houston Heights Polka* dedicated to My Friend, Col. N. L. Mills, Superintendent of Real Estate, Omaha and South Texas Land Company" and published the sheet music in 1893 in Houston. The cover had an elaborate drawing of "Hotel" which seems to be essentially the ground plan of the Company's real hotel, but with enough added spires and towers to make it look like a castle on the Rhine.

STREETS

In general the streets were named for c o l l e g e s and universities and in instances show the background of the men who developed the Heights. Ashland College was in Ashland, Ohio, but the name *Ashland* to Mr. Carter and Mr. Cooley must have meant back home in Nebraska. Some of the streets from Yale west to Lawrence and from Harvard east to Oxford carry out this idea of names for colleges. And one street, Portland, was later changed by city ordinance to a university name, Tulane.

Houston Heights is possibly the only old addition near Houston where the streets were laid out to vary only six degrees from true north and south. Mr. Cooley was chiefly responsible for planning the Boulevard and that street remains his great memorial. It is the oldest street in the vicinity of Houston which has needed no change in 65 years to widen its service area nor enhance its beauty, with its original esplanade in the middle and one-way thoroughfare on each side.

It is doubtful that in this part of the Gulf Coast country any other street has received as much notice for its natural beauty and its fortunate landscaping. Time and again the Boulevard scores the leading picture in the Sunday magazine section of Houston newspapers. One article deals with "then and now" centered about the fact that most of the pine trees have vanished. Another showed springtime blossoming of the "willow oaks" that "some old-timers called . . . pin oaks."

The latest article, by Sigman Byrd (*Houston Chronicle,* May 10, 1955) paid homage to "The Most Beautiful Street in Old Houston or the New" and showed the Boulevard resplendent in its glory of new street lights.

Long ago when ostrich feathers (the bigger the better) and feather boas, and long skirts with frills, and soutache braid and lacy jabots for trimming, and new collars built up on wire supports, made m'lady something truly wonderful to

18

behold, why Sunday promenading (in carriage or on high heels) along the Boulevard was Houston's original concept of a Fifth Avenue's Easter Parade.

STREET CARS

Mr. Carter's first step toward laying out his huge tract of land had been to guarantee transportation from Houston to the Heights. He had bought out the mule-drawn cars owned by H. F. MacGregor, which were later converted into electric street cars. We find C. A. McKinney, a Carter associate, first listed in the *City Directory 1892-1893* as "Sec'y and treas. H C St Ry Co," and in the next directory with the added "Bayou City Ry Co." In a business publication called *Industrial Advantages of Houston, Texas and Environs,* 1894, we find the Houston City Street Railway Company had incorporated in October, 1876, and that "when it came into the hands of the present management in 1890," it started something, "electrifying power to substitute for horses and mules." And "all the cars run upon a central belt in the center of the city..." With Mr. Carter as owner of the electric company, Mr. McKinney's position becomes significant of the power that built the Heights. It was good transportation from the very beginning that insured success for Mr. Carter's suburb.

Then on April 29, 1893, records show a deed from the Omaha and South Texas Land Company to the Houston Heights Street Railway Company setting out the right-of-way for the single track on either side of the esplanade, the east side turning on Boulevard to run west on 19th Avenue to Railroad Street, then south on Railroad to 17th Avenue and back to the west side of the esplanade on Boulevard.

The first motorman of the first street car to the Heights was Mr. Frank Wisnoski who remembers when the cars sometimes went out Railroad Street on the railroad tracks to the industries around 25th Avenue. Mr. Wisnoski says that often a box car would be left on the spur track of the railroad and thus hold up the street car. The company finally changed the route so that the cars turned down Ashland from 19th to 17th and avoided any use of the railroad tracks. A shuttle then was added to the service to run out to the industries.

Mention here should be made of Sam Danna, who for years was the best loved man on the Heights line. Sam went to work in 1907 and old-timers can remember how as children they would pass up others and wait for Sam Danna's car. The people of the Heights paid compliment to their favorite when the *Houston Chronicle* ran a popularity contest for street car conductors. Coupons for votes were cut from the newspapers. Fifty conductors entered the race. In the back of the Nineteenth Avenue Drug Store, Sam's managers spent hours cutting out the coupons, and every child in the Heights was scouring the neighborhood for extra papers. On February 1, 1913, Sam Danna won, with 959,480 votes to his credit.

HOUSTON HEIGHTS HOTEL

At the end of his car line, on the northeast corner of 19th and Ashland, Mr. Carter built the old Houston Heights Hotel. The hotel then meant to the Heights what a single skyscraper today means to an ambitious small town. A business center developed there at Ashland and 19th, and that corner was known as "the Heights." No record of the hotel has been discovered, but history of the place has been unearthed. Miss Nellie Kennedy is responsible for most of the details here given. She was living with her parents, Mr. and Mrs. M. W. Kennedy, in Pearland in 1897, when a family there who had run the hotel for Carter suggested that the Kennedys take over the management. In 1898, the change was made and in February, 1899, Miss Kennedy's brother came down from Iowa to assist his parents.

They opened the entire ground floor of the west wing for a dance hall. Mrs. Lottie Peacock remembers very "elegant" affairs being given there. The first floor of the east wing was the dining room. Parlors were on the second floor. In the spring of 1899 all rooms were rented for the summer and business seemed particularly promising for the Kennedy family. Miss Kennedy remembers only keen disappointment then, when Mr. Carter announced that he was thinking of selling. Actually he leased the hotel to Doctors Thornton and Davis. (This was the first time that any old settler had linked these two names with the change of the hotel to a medical center. Later P. V. Myers substantiated this statement.)

Miss Kennedy remembers that some of the soldiers, recruits for the Spanish-American War, in tent encampments around 4th and Boulevard, often came to the hotel for breakfast and dinner. One officer roomed and boarded there. O. M. Carter lived there, as did Mr. Stanley, who managed the water works. Dr. Fuller and his wife, and a Miss Yolland, a nurse, lived at the hotel. Miss Kennedy says that board and room ran about $3.50 per week, with a high rate of $5.00 for the best rooms.

OPERA HOUSE

In listing the improvements and attractions of the new addition to Houston, all the early advertisements for the Heights mention an opera house or theater located near the hotel. Mrs. Irene McBride (Houston Heights first postmaster) tells what she remembers concerning this place of amusement. It was called Houston Heights Opera House and was situated between Ashland and the water works on Railroad, on the north side of 19th Avenue. It was, therefore, opposite the McBride store and post office. And since it was an open-air theater, Mrs. McBride and her friends could sit on her upstairs porch, above the store, and see the show from good gallery seats. Because of its peculiar structure, only summer entertainment was provided. And even this schedule was irregular, possible only when the management could catch a troupe on circuit.

Usually the program was mediocre, if not really poor. However, on occasion an unusual circumstance gave the place a good show. Mrs. McBride remembers that the

21

National Band of Mexico played at the Heights Opera House about 1897, and the crowds were impressive because the music was worthwhile.

THE SALOON

Farther up 19th Avenue from McBride's store and across from the water works was a saloon. The saloon keeper owned a monkey named Jennie Yon Yon. On Sunday afternoons the place sponsored a balloon ascension when a man with his parachute and Jennie in one of her own took to the air. Crowds gathered to watch the ascension, and Jennie made a name for herself in the 19th Avenue center of the Heights. One day Jennie appeared without ceremony in the office of D. D. Cooley, in the southwest corner of Carter's Hotel. Mr. Cooley found Jennie perched on top of his desk licking the brush from his mucilage pot. That day Jennie got "stuck up."

During Mayor Barker's term of office, the saloons were driven out when the Heights was voted dry on September 25, 1912. The Heights already had half a dozen saloons and the residents wanted these removed from the vicinity of their homes. The matter was never a question of Pros and Antis. The electioneering, Mayor Barker recalls, was all carried on at night, because that was the only time that anybody could spare for the business. It was all kept free of politics and remained to the end a matter of homeowners protecting their neighborhoods from disturbing influences.

The dry law in the Heights is still enforced. And the question of boundaries affected by the law comes more frequently to the Heights Library for solution than any other purely local inquiry. Here are the boundaries as quoted by Mayor Barker to the Heights Library:

> From White Oak Bayou and Heights Boulevard to the west line of the Heights plat — north to 16th Street — west to west line of Houston Heights plat — north to center of 26th Street — east down center of 26th Street to center of Yale Street — south on center of Yale Street to center of 22nd Street — east on center of 22nd Street to east end of

Heights plat again — then south following east line
Heights Addition to White Oak Bayou — following bayou
to Heights Boulevard.

BRIDGES

Houston Illustrated . . . 1893 gives details on the bridges
that linked the Heights to Houston. Across the bayou on
the Boulevard there were twin bridges, 60 feet apart, 45 feet
wide, and 250 feet long. They were built on cedar pilings,
nine feet abreast. Each bridge took 65,000 feet of lumber,
so "solidly put together" that any vehicle or weight could
be sustained. The next notation is evidence of the determination of the land company to insure the beauty of its
main street: "One (bridge) would have sufficed but two
were necessary to maintain uniformity of the Boulevard."

THE RAILROAD

Again we get history from *Houston Illustrated:* "The
Houston Heights steam railway . . . extends the entire length
of the Heights with side tracks and switches throughout the
streets and alleys in the manufacturing districts . . ."

THE RAILROAD STATION

As early as 1895 the *City Directory* gives the M. K. and
T. Railroad Station in the Heights as "3 miles from Houston." In 1954 it still operated. A long passenger train
would stop at 7th and Yale and tie up traffic on across
Boulevard and Harvard. At night the people in cars were
halted to see the conductor, waving his lantern, descend,
put his little steps in place, and help maybe one or two
passengers to alight. Mission accomplished, the conductor
put back his steps, officially swung his lantern, as if it were
a censer doing homage to the Heights, and signalled the
train (and waiting traffic) to move on.

Before 1913 the Heights station seemingly was just a
building by the side of the road, on 7th and Allston. The
Suburbanite on April 18, 1913, gave the following article
with the headline as is:

23

HOUSTON HEIGHTS ON THE MAP

The station house on the Missouri, Kansas and Texas Railway has been cleaned up, repainted, and provided with seats for patrons. It looks very much like a railway station indeed.

The sign "Houston Heights" in great big letters is in conspicuous places at the east and west ends of the building.

This is the first time Houston Heights has been recognized by any railroad and thus we get on the map. The Katy did it.

In answer to an inquiry regarding the history of this station, the following information was received from M. R. Cring, Assistant to President, M. K. and T. Lines, St. Louis:

We find little information in our records concerning the old city of Houston Heights. When our track was constructed into Houston in 1893, we crossed the railroad going out Nicholson (then Railroad) Street. It was owned at that time by the Houston Railway Company. D. D. Cooley was President and C. A. McKinney was Secretary of that Company. We also find it referred to as Houston Heights Steam Railway. It was later taken over by the Houston and Texas Central...

Our original Houston Heights Station was a frame building near the corner of 7th and Allston, constructed in 1895. In 1920 this station was enlarged and converted to a section house and a small brick and stucco station erected on Seventh between Yale and Heights Boulevard. This station was removed in 1954.

ELECTRIC LIGHTS

On September 23, 1905 the *Suburbanite,* on page 1 ran an impressive advertisement announcing that the Houston Heights Electric Company "will soon be ready to furnish electricity to the people of the Heights." And earlier still, on January 28, 1905, in its first issue, the paper had put this item in its local news column: "Coombs Terrace will soon be lighted by electric lights."

Before that time residents who were near enough to the trolley line could get electric lights from the power of the street car service. But, Miss Helen Milroy remembers, every time the car passed, the lights dimmed.

ICE PLANT

An interesting advertisement appears on the back of an old political pamphlet of early Houston Heights. The details give a good social perspective of early life in the Heights:

HEIGHTS ICE PLANT
26th and Ashland

SOUTH TEXAS COTTON OIL COMPANY

Please remember that we deliver ice without extra cost to you ALL WINTER . . . ANYBODY can sell ice cheap in SUMMERTIME and then sell their mules, discharge their workmen, and let you whistle for ice in wintertime.
DON'T patronize the irresponsible wagons . . .

WATERWORKS

One block west of the hotel, on 19th and Ashland, Mr. Carter put up his power plant for his waterworks, on 19th and Railroad. For years the grounds were kept like a park and even today the grounds at the plant add a note of cool relief from the dusty, busy life of West 19th Avenue.

HOMES AND FIRST SETTLERS

Located on the southwest corner of 16th and Ashland, the first two lots sold by Carter's Realty Company were bought by a carpenter for the company, S. D. Wilkins, who built his home there and who later became the second postmaster of the Heights. The first home built by the Omaha and South Texas Land Company, in 1893, was the Cooley home at 1802 Boulevard. Today (1955) it is still standing and occupied by Mr. and Mrs. Arthur Cooley.

Mr. and Mrs. D. D. Cooley, with their three little boys, Denton, Arthur, and Ralph, moved in when the building was only partially finished. Arthur Cooley remembers hearing his mother tell of keeping the children upstairs because of prowling wolves before the neighborhood was built up.

A block from the Cooleys, also on Heights Boulevard, C. A. McKinney built his home. Each of the Carter associates in turn erected a fine house on the east side of the Boulevard. The reason for c h o o s i n g that side was the fact that only on the east side of the esplanade did the street have shell surfacing. The only home of any of the group that was sold was the N. L. Mills house, between 15th and 16th on the Boulevard, which about 1894 became the home of Nelson A. Baker. After 1901 the house belonged to the H. A. Paine family, and then after 1908 for about thirty years was the home of the W. A. McNeill family, long p r o m i n e n t in Heights history. John A. Milroy at first resided at 16th and Harvard, and before 1898 moved his family to the home at 1102 Boulevard which he had bought from H. F. McGregor. The home is still o w n e d by Mr. Milroy's daughter, Helen.

All of these old homes had the popular cupola of the period and the gabled roof to top off the elegant decoration. The Mills home was possibly the most pretentious, highly decorative with its intricate "gingerbread" fretwork. One pictures lace curtains, the tea cozy, and the tray for calling cards as setting the tone for early Boulevard society.

Only Carter of the group at first made no home for himself, but after his second marriage in 1920, he lived in the big house at 1316 Boulevard. That home in 1893 is pictured in a view book as the residence of William Shannon, a real estate agent. Shannon himself seems to have left behind an aura of great elegance. One early settler says that Mr. Shannon's real estate office was truly a grand reception room. The caller presented his card and was formally received (or discouraged) and without the card had little chance of any notice. The Shannon home was built of the finest lumber and with the best possible cabinet work. But by 1894 the Shannon family had left the Heights and the family of the Rev. Benjamin A. Rogers occupied the home. The house later became known to old-timers as the Tempest home, due to the fact that Mrs. Tempest, a prominent woman in the Heights and a daughter of the Rev. and Mrs. B. A. Rogers, lived there. In 1907, for a time, it was leased to Purdy Sanitarium. It seems likely that this house, which after 1920 finally became known as the Carter home, was first erected in connection with Carter interests, although there is no proof of any relationship between Shannon and Carter.

William Peacock, from New York, had been persuaded by Mr. Carter to come to Texas in 1893. With his bride, Mr. Peacock planned a home at 16th and Harvard and later moved the house to 1401 Boulevard. In 1955, Mrs. Lottie Peacock, now a widow, is probably the oldest resident who has continuously lived on Heights Boulevard. Her home was the second built on the west side of the esplanade.

The first was the home of John L. Garwood, located on the southwest corner of 16th. It is quite probable that the house was built by Carter. At any rate, the Garwood family left the Heights about 1897.

From 1894 until 1898, John T. Boyle and his father were proprietors of the famous Hutchins House in Houston. O. M. Carter had boarded there. John T. Boyle also engaged in the real estate business. This mutual interest sealed a friendship between the two men, and usually Carter led his friends to the Heights. In 1898, therefore, the Boyle family moved into the vacated Garwood home. Except for a short period away from the Heights, this family remained for years prominent in Heights affairs.

FACTORIES AND BUSINESS DEVELOPMENT

The Industrial Advantages of Houston, Texas and Environs in 1894 is authority that the Houston General Electric Company of Houston Heights was founded October, 1892 and incorporated as a stock company on May 5, 1893. The president was Scott Van Etten and the secretary-treasurer was L. M. Kilburn. It is i n t e r e s t i n g to note that both these men were from Omaha. The l e n g t h y entry in the business publication cites enough evidence to show that the company of electrical engineers, contractors, and manufacturers had "installed lighting" plants all over Texas and the "entire l i g h t i n g plant and wiring for Houston Heights." (The fly in the ointment here would seem to be the fact that Heights citizens had no lights until 1905, twelve years later.) According to the books, the Omaha interest was no small business. *The City of Houston,* 1893, specifies $30,000 capital of the company "for the manufacture of electrical specialties." The concern built its plant between 24th and 25th on Railroad, and a photograph exists of the imposing building. Most likely the panic of 1893 hit this business as it did all others.

Just north, across the street from the Electric Company, on 25th and Railroad and running back to Lawrence, was the A. J. Wheeler Furniture Company, which according to *The City of Houston,* 1893, had capital "$100,000, capacity 600 chamber suites per month, in addition to other lines of furniture." Other than this entry in a book, no further evidence was discovered of actual production.

This one-story extensive plant apparently changed its first purpose because it later manufactured compo-board, and compo-board in turn made history for the Heights. The product is said to have been the first compressed wall board made in the United States. The factory sent out by the thousands small sample blocks of its product, mailed through the Houston Heights Post Office, with a 2¢ stamp on each postcard sample. This big boost to cancellations for the Heights Post Office caused officials to make inquiry and then to determine to divert "all this business" to the downtown office. That effort failed. Then the authorities tried to change the name of the post office. It was humiliating that such a bulk of business should be credited to the new post office station. But O. M. Carter was personally acquainted with President William McKinley and the matter was taken to the White House and settled to the satisfaction of the Heights Post Office.

This all happened before the end of 1897. Mrs. Irene McBride is authority for the details, and she resigned as postmaster in that year. In 1955, Mrs. McBride is still living and active as one of Houston Heights' oldest and best-loved citizens.

After the compo-board experiment, the building at 25th and Railroad housed its most successful venture, the Pickle Factory. After two fires and many vicissitudes, a part of the old plant still remains, and on the site today is a venetian blind industry.

A block south of the Houston General Electric Company and the original furniture company's building stood a planing mill, across the street from where Helms School is now located. Here on the sidetrack of the railroad that Carter had switched out on the street that is now called Nicholson, material could conveniently be assembled and shipped. The sawmill took care of the immense amount of lumber from trees felled in laying out streets. Its capacity was 20,000 feet a day, and many homes in the Heights were built from lumber prepared in the neighborhood.

If the homes needed brick, that, too, was handy. On the corner of 4th and Yale, on the railroad (which does not turn off Yale until it reaches 6th) was located the Houston Brick and Tile Company "in full operation" in 1893, with a capital stock of $30,000.

According to *The City of Houston* . . . 1893, the Houston Car Company (called the Car Works) had "capital of $400,000 and capacity of 28 cars a day." No real evidence could be found that the car works actually turned out any cars.* But the photograph of the building shows an imposing plant. Even before Carter sold his steam railroad and his street car interests (about 1895) this building had gradually

*Harris County Mortgage Records, vol. 23, p. 233, give deed of trust.

slipped out of the picture of transportation interests in the Heights.

A mattress factory with $30,000 invested was built on 22nd and Lawrence. This building, too, was diverted from its first purpose and converted into the Oriental Textile Mill. The mill proper took up the large block between 22nd and 23rd and between Lawrence and North Shepherd. The company built cottages on the block directly north of the plant for its employees, and the unit came to be known as the Textile Village. A spur of the railroad ran over from what is now known as Nicholson Street to accommodate the mill. B. J. Platt for years was superintendent of the plant that turned out a product which looked like long rolls of carpeting and which was used for pressing cotton seed oil. The plant's capacity was about 50 rolls a day, varying in price from $200 to $400 a roll.

The textile was woven from hair. Old residents of the Heights have handed down the story that in the beginning much of the hair was obtained from China when pigtails were being discarded. But certain it is that camel's hair in time came to be the staple used in production. Only within the last few years did the Textile Mill discontinue operation.

Farther out, on 26th and Railroad, was located the South Texas Cotton Oil Company. According to F. G. Brashear, who went to work there in 1907, the plant operated as the Roberts Cotton Oil Company. It was built around 1900, possibly earlier. A recorded deed shows that Roberts sold out on July 7, 1910, for $30,000 cash and three notes of $10,000 each, to the South Texas Cotton Oil Company. W. A. Sherman, who had been secretary of the Roberts Cotton Oil Company, then became president of the new firm.

There was an earlier cotton seed oil mill on 6th Street "in course of construction" in 1893, which was known as the Consumers Oil Mill, now called the Houston Oil Mill, and in 1955 a subsidiary of Swift and Company. The original company's capital was $500,000.*

STORES AND SMALL BUSINESS ENTERPRISES

There were two two-story brick business buildings opposite the big hotel on 19th and Ashland. In the one just beyond the southwest corner, Carter promised six months free rent to a young couple, the W. C. McBrides, if they would open a store. Carter wanted facilities for his new residents of the Heights. The McBrides agreed and their store, opened in 1893, is the first on record in the Heights. From the beginning, this store ties up with the history of the post office, and in 1896 it was the voting place for the election called to determine whether or not the community would incorporate as a municipality.

John L. Garwood, who lived on the southwest corner of 16th and Boulevard, followed the McBrides with a dry goods and grocery store, located on the southeast corner of 19th and Ashland. Garwood was also the first marshal, serving one term. In 1899 he is not listed in the *City Directory*.

Miss Nellie Kennedy, who helped to operate Carter's hotel from 1898 to 1899, remembers that William Backus had a store across from the hotel, possibly in the building vacated by Garwood. Backus is there in 1899, the year *City Directory* fails to list Garwood.

Mrs. Lottie Peacock is authority that her husband, William Peacock, built a small business house near the corner of 19th and Ashland and rented it to a Chinaman for a Chinese laundry. She says that the business lasted several years until about 1896.

*The Heights Library a number of years ago came into possession of some excellent photos of early industries taken about 1901 and including pictures of the Hotel, the Car Works, the Houston General Electric Company, the Planing Mill, and the Consumers Oil Mill.

The first substantial merchandise business that left behind a long record of service was the A. J. Myers store, opened on August 12, 1902, on the southeast corner of 9th and Yale. For years Myers Store, wholesale and retail, groceries and feed department, including a meat market, covered the whole territory of the Heights. Later, stores in different localities drew neighborhood trade. Wimberly's on 7th, set back from the Boulevard, was for a long time the gathering place for that section of the Heights. S. J. Wimberly (known to old-timers as Spot Wimberly) was for years tax collector, and people paid their taxes at the store on 7th until the Fire Station and City Hall was built in 1914. Odd about payment of those taxes: before Wimberly G. W. Wilson was Tax Assessor and Collector and people paid at the Wilson home at 7½ Oxford or had Mr. Wilson call to collect.

Stores played a great part in building the community, especially those around the center called "the Heights." After 1900 there were at that location, in addition to the Nineteenth Avenue Drug Store on the southeast corner of 19th and A s h l a n d, McDonald's Grocery Store, Lewis's Grocery, Ernest Long's Store, and Trautwein's Meat Market.

One early customer remembers that Trautwein's Market was particularly clean. It had the freshly scrubbed look that one associates with a Dutch kitchen. A big sign on the wall was significant: "If you spit on the floor at home, spit on the floor here. We want you to feel at home." The atmosphere in the store was likewise as homey as in a kitchen. The average child then was simple in the sense of being unaware of the clever sayings that today make him wise at an early age. Then he would say in a wheedling voice, "Mr. Trautwein gimme a weenie?" And Mr. Trautwein, grumbling, but well aware that the youngster would u n d e r s t a n d, would hand down a weiner as if it were an apple.

The Trautwein family and the McDonald family lived over their business houses, but many stores had halls on the second floors. The Presbyterian Church for a time held services over Frank Johnson's drug store, and the Baptist Temple started over the Lewis store. Moreover, Cooley School's two classrooms occupied the upstairs of these same two stores when Cooley was remodeled into a larger building in 1906. Then, too, the first medical center (as such) was located in the top story of the same drug store. Fred Dexter's Department Store, on 17th and Rutland, lent its second story for meetings. Later still, Whiteside's Store on 18th and Ashland also contributed in this way when Fraternal Hall burned and made necessary some other community center.

The G. A. Maack family were active in the social and civic life of the Heights after 1900. They had the Heights Meat Market at 346 West 19th. Their old ad appears in the advertising section of the *Houston Heights Charter,* and after their routine announcement they add "Green Ground Bone for Chickens."

F. F. Ibsch, on 22nd and Yale had a grocery and general merchandise store listed in the *City Directory 1908-1909.* In 1912, Mr. and Mrs. Dave Kaplan leased the Ibsch store for two years. In 1914 the Kaplans purchased the property across the street from Ibsch and built their own business house with living quarters above the store.

Today Kaplan's and Ben Hur Department Store is located on the original plot of ground, and is one of the very few early stores that has continued in business. It is still owned and operated by the Dave Kaplan family.

R. T. Mumme, at 13th and Rutland, is entered in the phone book in 1911. H. P. Guinn and Son, at 112 West 8th, ran big advertisements in the *Suburbanite* around 1912.

One odd custom that has died out was the daily visitation from the grocery store. Every morning the grocery man (and nobody said grocer man) came to the back door, not because that door was his proper place but because he followed that custom. Perhaps because the lady of the

33

house in the morning would be in the kitchen. At any rate, he got the list for the day and later delivered the groceries. Nobody *shopped* for groceries, and only the children were chased to the store for what their mother forgot to order. One time a little girl had climbed up on the roof of the barn and was afraid to look down, much less to come down. She simply stayed on the roof y e l l i n g. The worried mother waited for the grocery man, had the ladder ready, and the good Samaritan fixed everything. The grocery man even got kids down off the roof.

THE BAKERY

At the end of the year 1905, the *Suburbanite* mentions that Norregaard's Bakery has a "new enlarged oven." No early resident of the Heights who once tasted Norregaard's bread could ever forget it. The bakery was back of the Norregaard home on Portland, between 15th and 16th. At first Mr. Norregaard peddled his bread in a basket. Then he got a horse and buggy. On Saturdays he started out around eleven o'clock, with c i n n a m o n rolls that left behind a delicious odor and which made the baker something of a pied piper. On more than one occasion children ran after the flying horse and buggy, trying to catch up with the tempting cinnamon rolls, which for "5¢ worth" were very filling. It is possible that Mr. Norregaard drove fast because his supply was limited to his regular c u s t o m e r s. The bakery never grew into a big plant and the bread never changed from its homemade quality.

THE HEIGHTS A REAL ESTATE PROPOSITION

All the factories, stores and small business enterprises were encouraged because to O. M. Carter a new town was in the making, and the people who would locate in his town needed facilities. But his undertaking was essentially a real estate proposition. He had laid out, according to one authority, 11,000 lots. It is interesting then to notice that many of the outstanding men whom most certainly Carter, or his company, influenced to move to the Heights, were real

estate men. Many of them, for instance Wm. A. Wilson and
D. Barker, would open up additions in other sections of
Houston.

One of them never moved to the Heights, but acquired
interest in Heights property through other negotiations, as
in the securities involved in Carter's street car transactions
with H. F. MacGregor. One or two of them engaged in other
business and made real estate merely their investment
consideration. The early *Suburbanite* mentions house after
house built by some of these men who had faith in the
Heights. The history of the Heights then is a history of
land.

Besides the original group of men associated with the
Omaha and South Texas Land Company, others prominent
in this story of real estate were: William Shannon, Nelson
A. Baker, William Peacock, Eden L. Coombs, P. M. Gran-
berry, John T. Boyle, Wm. A. Wilson, D. Barker, and W. A.
McNeill.

THE

GOVERNMENT

OMAHA AND SOUTH TEXAS LAND COMPANY LIQUIDATES

Sometime in 1895, the Omaha and South Texas Land Company liquidated its holdings and divided its assets. About this time, Carter also negotiated the sale of the street car company.

Mr. Cooley, who had been the treasurer and trustee, then devoted himself to his private real estate and his other interests, finally making insurance his chief business. Mr. McKinney, who had been the company's director of the street car and transit end of the Heights venture, after 1895 became associated with the South Texas Commercial and National Bank.

Mr. Carter, after closing the books on the division of properties, bought up shares of all who wished to sell and prepared to operate under the simple name of Houston Heights. But Mr. Carter never had assumed the direction of the real estate development. He was the financial head who interested outside capital investment and who was able from his own resources to lend security to his undertaking. He, therefore, needed a sound real estate man to remain as manager of his properties and thus John Milroy became the only one of the original group who stayed on with Mr. Carter.

It is doubtful if many people who moved to the Heights after 1895 ever heard of the Omaha and South Texas Land Company. They remember only

HOUSTON HEIGHTS OFFICE
O. M. Carter, Owner
John A. Milroy, Agent and Manager

A MUNICIPALITY EMERGES

In the early days of the development of the Heights, the Omaha and South Texas Land Company controlled the affairs of its property. It expended more than a half million dollars, as its advertisement says "in cold cash" (and records substantiate the statement) for improvements before a "single lot was offered for sale." The money was spent for clearing and grading the streets, in constructing a steam railroad for the manufacturing industries, for its electric street railway, and for the erection of buildings.

But once lots were sold, the situation changed and the needs of the community became the concern of the new property owners. Moreover, the company itself had led the way to a new development when it dissolved its corporate holdings. A new incorporation then became a necessity. On June 18, 1896, H. D. Brooke and more than 19 other residents filed in the office of the County Judge application to have incorporated Houston Heights Municipality. On June 18, 1896 the County Judge ordered an election to be held at McBride's Store on July 1, 1896. At that election 87 votes in favor of and 10 opposed to incorporation were cast. Thus the Heights became incorporated as a "village" under chapter 11, title 18, of the Revised Statutes of Texas and assumed its own municipal government, with mayor, aldermen, assessor, tax collector, and marshal. It levied, collected, and controlled its own taxes, and the minutes of the Heights council meetings, with the record of its deliberations actually make up a history of the Heights.

When by annexation the Heights in 1918 became a part of the City of Houston, these records were turned over to the downtown City Hall. In the new City Hall building they are available, except the ledger for the years 1903-1911. That one could not be found in June, 1955, but as the assistant explained, "It could be here, but mixed up with other old records like it."

The first ledger covers from August 24, 1896 to March 3, 1903. The minutes are written in the fine script of C. A. McKinney, E. W. Leman, J. L. Garwood, John A. Milroy, and J. D. Lyons. Not a historical fact, but a great pleasure to record: no erasure, no error in spelling or composition was found in the lengthy account of each meeting. Would that penmanship today could be directed to those model forms! Mayor W. G. Love presided at the first meeting and administered the oath of office to the "several aldermen elect": John A. Milroy, E. Hanson, F. J. Steger, F. C. Van Liew, and C. A. McKinney. There is no record to indicate the manner of Mayor Love's own election or installation.

At this first meeting two motions were made and carried; for appointment of a committee to see to an engineer's survey of boundaries of the municipality and for the fixing of $3,000 bond for the marshal. In the deed records of Harris County, vol. 97, p. 365, we find "Field notes of boundaries of corporation of Houston Heights, J. O. Davis, C. E., acknowledged 19 March, 1897." And "Corrected field notes" by the same engineer acknowledged June 4, 1897, can be found in Deed Records of Harris County, vol. 105, pp. 499-500. Here is evidence that the council acted without delay upon its recommendations and decisions.

The election of public officials was held annually and both the minutes for April 19, 1897, and for April 23, 1898, record the reelection of W. G. Love for mayor, with slight variation in the choice of aldermen. G. A. Lund, D. D. Cooley, and J. L. Garwood went into office in 1897, and E. S. Pierson replaced Lund in 1898.

J. L. Garwood had been the first marshal, and when he resigned in 1897, G. W. Wilson succeeded him and remained in office for years.

On April 4, 1899, the returns of the election are given and a complete change of officials is noticed. John A. Milroy became the new mayor, with A. T. Parker, T. V. West, J. M. Limbocker, Charles Schuler, E. Dietrich, and G. A. Lund elected as aldermen. The first ledger of minutes of council meetings closes March 3, 1903, and each April for four years before that date shows Milroy's return to office. The *Houston Chronicle* fills in for the missing records to show that on the first Tuesday of April, 1907, David Barker was elected to succeed Mr. Milroy, who had served 8 years.

Because of missing records it seemed impossible to state definitely when the annual election gave way to the pattern for a two-year term of office.

And then Mrs. L. R. Smith (Garnet Robinson to old-timers) brought a copy of the *Houston Heights Charter,* dated 1911, to the Heights Library. In section 16, page 27, the reason for a new or revised Charter is asserted:

> The fact that the municipality of Houston Heights has no adequate charter, but is operating under the general statutes of the State of Texas, and is unable from its present revenues to provide adequate police and fire protection, and its taxing powers, under the general laws, are wholly insufficient for the needs of said city, creates an emergency and an imperative public necessity that the constitutional rule requiring bills to be read on three several days be suspended and the same is hereby suspended and this Act shall take effect and be in force from and after its passage, and it is so enacted.
>
> Approved March 2, 1911
> Became a law March 2, 1911.

And on page 17 is noted the change from an annual election of officers:

...On the first Tuesday in April, 1911...and on the first Tuesday in April each succeeding two years thereafter, an election shall be held...at which all the officers... shall be elected.

The second book of minutes of the council that is available today dates from 1911 to 1914 and then two other books cover December 7, 1914 to April 2, 1917, and from April 10, 1917, to February 26, 1918.

Piecing together all evidence from different sources, the records show the highest office in the Heights municipality to have been held by the following mayors:—

W. G. Love	1896 to April, 1899	3 Years
John A. Milroy	1899 to April, 1907	8 years
D. Barker	1907 to April, 1913	6 years
R. F. Isbell	1913 to Aug. 4, 1914	1 year, 5 months
J. B. Marmion	Sept. 5, 1914 to	
	Feb. 26, 1918	3 years, 5 months

Mr. Isbell's business connections made it necessary for him to move to Taft, Texas, and resign from office as mayor on August 4, 1914. During the absence of Mayor Isbell, Earl Wilson had acted as mayor pro tem. His record during that time entitles him to a place in this history. Mr. Wilson was perhaps the youngest man in the circle of citizens responsible for the local government and his ability was recognized by his associates. When the special election was held on September 5, 1914, J. B. Marmion, the new Mayor, found his office in good order.

In the history of elections in the Heights, the oddest feature of human interest is noticed in April, 1900. From Mayor Milroy on down to the last alderman, each name is credited with 37 votes.

The history of Houston Heights is interesting in the light of comparative evaluation as far as finance is concerned. The study of the American dollar involves a study of history. The written records of the Heights prove that Judge Love as mayor and his first councilmen were anything but mediocre; they were outstanding men in the City of Houston and in the State of Texas. Their deliberations in council meeting, therefore, are not typical of what we find on the agenda in small hamlets that sprang up in many pioneering communities. That fact makes it all the more interesting to note some of the recorded data expressive of an age that counted pennies and s c r u p u l o u s l y avoided waste. One man presented a bill and

> the bill...for seventy-five cents for ink provided by him for Cooley School was allowed and a warrant drawn in payment of same.

Every expenditure was entered:

> Jno. Grant for removing *Dd.* Hog, 102 Yale...25¢

This item has a check mark to indicate payment of the 25¢. As late as August 4, 1914, acting Mayor Earl Wilson wished

> ...to ascertain the opinion of the other members of the council on the question of allowing...to maintain two extra cows on lots near his home.

The minutes are entered with great precision and exacttitude, and then the ledger falls into the hands of some person wielding a heavy lead pencil and writing a scrawling hand. At this point, two pages give a table of contents to ordinances, arranged alphabetically. The following is indicative of what seemed necessary legislation:—

> 425 Portland Street Ordinance changing Name to Tulane
> 236 Peddlers to Secure License
> 244 Privy Clean
> 312 Striking Matches
> 315 Spitting on Floor City Hall
> 235 Train Jumping

And then in comparison to those early q u e s t i o n s of finance originating in council meetings, we find in 1911, bonds to the amount of $180,000 "were recently voted by a majority of more than five to one, to macadamize eight miles of cross streets," and "to pave both sides of the Boulevard with brick." (One newspaper article stated a number of years ago that the Boulevard was paved in 1907 and other articles since then have repeated this error.)

One thing is certain, the history of Houston Heights as a municipality is a record of absolute integrity. The government so well ruled its own affairs that it was free of debt and owned its public utilities when it came into the City of Houston. On February 20, 1918, Houston and the Heights voted to incorporate Carter's old suburb into a greater Houston. The last meeting of the Heights Council was held February 26, 1918.

ANNEXATION IN 1918

J. B. Marmion was mayor and other officers of the Heights Municipality at that time were: Councilmen M. L. O. Andrews, J. T. Boyle, Charles Hawkins, C. J. Trautwein; James G. Donovan, City Attorney; H. C. Colley, Recorder; L. L. McFee, City Marshal; S. J. Wimberly, Assessor and Collector; H. Montgomery, Fire Chief.

POST OFFICE

The late Mrs. Pearl Hendricks contributed many articles on the history of Houston and its environs to local newspapers, and all her writing was marked by meticulous care in composition and painstaking accuracy in statement of fact. On June 27, 1937, the *Houston Chronicle* ran a full page account of her story of the Heights Post Office, and on April 3, 1939, the *Houston Post* gave another story by Mrs. Hendricks of "The Perambulating Post Office of Heights...History Filled with Pioneer Names." Both newspaper articles have been preserved in the scrapbook at the Heights Library.

Mrs. Hendricks interviewed all the early postmasters except Mr. Wilkins, who had died. However, she did see Mrs. Percy O. Endt, Mr. Wilkins' daughter, who had assisted her father at the post office. Any historian of the Heights must be grateful to Mrs. Hendricks for her timely notes because she and nearly all those early appointees (with the notable exception of the first, Mrs. McBride) are now dead in 1955, and there was no written record of the history of the post office before Mrs. Hendricks' article. The following outline in this present work is almost wholly dependent upon information supplied by Mrs. Hendricks.

When in 1893, Mr. Carter arranged for Mr. and Mrs. W. C. McBride to operate a store on the southwest corner of Ashland and 19th, he also planned to have mail delivered at that outpost. Mrs. McBride recalls letters being kept in a cigar box on the counter so that folks could look for their own mail. Then came the formal appointment of Mrs. McBride as postmaster of Houston Heights on July 7, 1894. Mrs. McBride served three years and then resigned in 1897.

S. D. Wilkins was appointed postmaster on August 7, 1897. His daughter, Mrs. P. O. Endt, remembered that he served as postmaster in an office in Garwood's grocery and feed store. She also remembered clerks during her father's ten-year term; Miss Katie Pratt, Miss Louise Quinn, and Mrs. Lea McCormick. While Mr. Wilkins served, the post office was moved twice, from Garwood's store back to its original location in the building that the McBride's had vacated, and then to a different store in the same block.

One error crept into the post office history as related by Mrs. Endt to Mrs. Hendricks. The account reads "During the Spanish-American War, old Highland Park, now Woodland Playground, was converted into a training camp. Postmaster Wilkins of Houston Heights got permission to collect all outgoing mail, letters written by the soldier boys and by the officers. His daughter, Mrs. Endt, says: 'That was a big help, too, because the office was still fourth class, paying only in cancellations.'" Mrs. Endt must have referred to Coombs Park, or Forest Park as it was sometimes called, where soldiers of the Fourth Texas Regiment were located at Camp Tom Ball.

After Mr. Wilkins, Mrs. Emma F. Ellis (who was later Mrs. R. C. Harris and in 1938 Mrs. George Mitchell) was appointed postmaster in 1907. She took over office when mail was handled in a room in Ernest Long's store on the north side of West 19th, about midway between Ashland and Carter's park at the waterworks.

Mrs. Ellis resigned in 1910, and H. G. Whiteside was appointed her successor. The new postmaster had built an imposing, two-story frame department store on 18th and Ashland, and here he located the post office. The building burned about 1912 and Mr. Whiteside moved from the Heights.

J. J. Hill became the new postmaster. He, too, had a new two-story store building in which to locate the post office. Here, on the south side of 19th, across the street from Ernest Long's store, Mr. Hill served for a short time. And then T. J. Long was appointed and moved the post office to its early location in the Ernest Long store.

Then, on October 1, 1913, John Dunlop was appointed postmaster, and the old store-keeper and postmaster combination went out of style. Mr. Dunlop moved around the corner to the rear of Fulton's Drug Store building and arranged the post office to face Ashland.

On March 1, 1915, the Heights Post Office was made into a sub-station of the Houston office and Postmaster Dunlop became the first superintendent of the station. (Later Mr. Dunlop was to become the Postmaster of the City of Houston.)

In December, 1917, Mr. Dunlop was transferred to the downtown post office, and on January 1, 1918, R. R. Royall took over the management of the Heights sub-station. Mr. Royall would, like Mr. Dunlop, attain high position in the postal service, but this history of the Heights ends its tracings with annexation in February, 1918.

JAILS

On 18th, between Ashland and Railroad, on the south side of the street, the community built the jail. Never very successful, with no booming business back of it, the jail was housed in a two-story, red brick building.* About 1906 it was a forlorn-looking, old empty house where children

---

* There is question about the building. Some old settlers insist that the jail was a one-story structure; others are just as certain that it was a two-story building. All agree on the location.

played in the vacant lots around it and looked through the iron bars into the lock-up room. For a time it was rented, and once there was a millinery shop in the front part of the downstairs floor.

When inquiries were made in 1955 of an old resident as to why the jail was not used, the reason given was: "Once a couple of drunks were thrown in, but the ants got at them and they hollered so much and raised so much sand that nobody ever got jailed there again." Asked what served next, the same informant said that the new fire station on 12th had a "private room for emergencies." Sure enough, at the back of the fire station, running along the Yale Street side, there is a *strong* room with an iron door and evidence where bars had been attached to the one window. Today there are only firemen's boots there.

One fireman said in 1955 that he remembered when Judge Olive held court in the room upstairs that today serves as a dormitory for the firemen. The guilty then got locked up right there at the station. All very handy. This Judge Olive was really Dr. William Olive, who served as City Recorder and who held court in that capacity.

The law enforcement officer who made the arrests when Judge Olive served was Webb Furlow. And before Mr. Furlow's term of office, G. W. Wilson, Tax Collector, acted as marshal. Mr. Wilson's son Clifton is still a resident of the Heights.

On Friday, October 13, 1913, the *Suburbanite* tells of court proceedings:

> Judge Olive did a full day's business last Friday in his court. There were three "pig stye" cases brought up before him but the defendants pleaded guilty to the hog pen charge and each paid a fine of $5 and the furbelows to the tune of $11. A man was also brought up for driving on the sidewalk. He wisely did not stand trial and pleaded guilty; his fine was $5, with the usual ornaments, all amounting to $16.

The following week the *Suburbanite* told of court with a novel headline for its article:

46

WHERE WERE YOUR VEGETABLES WASHED?

One day last week Joe Ross was brought before Recorder Wm. Olive on the charge of selling and offering for sale insanitary fruit and vegetables... Fined $5 and ornaments amounting to $16. This sum he left with Judge Olive, but he felt bad about it.

In an old box found some years ago by a newspaper woman hunting a story at the fire station, the Heights Library came into possession of a report made by Mayor Marmion for the year 1915. Marmion lists for the Police Department: "$50 for subsistence of prisoners," and adds another $20 for "Stationery." Odd ratio, but proof that not too many prisoners had to be fed.

The possible reason for combining the new fire station and the jail might have been the fact that the old jail on 18th was converted into a fire station. The converted building then did double service, as a pound for all lost animals, dogs, horses, mules, or whatever got away, and besides housed H. F. D., No. 13.

FIRE DEPARTMENT

Fire Fighters of Houston, by Chas. Green, 1915, traces the origin of the Heights Fire Department:

Volunteer fire service was instituted September 1, 1908 with a two-tank chemical engine. The company at once bought a lot and constructed a building on Yale Street between Ninth and Tenth Avenues. Dr. Gunn was president; H. M. Richter, secretary; C. J. Eisenhour, treasurer; Horace Olive, chief, who served two years of the volunteer regime. Dr. William Olive was the last president.

The volunteer fire department had no funds nor did it receive substantial recognition, so that after some time it sold the "chemical engine" to the Lufkin Township. The Heights Library now owns a picture of this first fire equipment, given by Horace Olive in 1955. The donor was a small boy riding with the fireman at the time the picture was taken. His uncle, the first fire chief, is driving the two horses, and on the wagon were representatives of the volunteer fire department.

A tax-supported fire department was set up in 1910, on 13th and Boulevard, behind the Durham home. The station opened out into what might be called the alley between the Boulevard and Yale, on the south side of 13th. Jay L. Durham was the first paid fire chief, and the firemen were: Lee Nixon, Lee Butler, Lloyd Glover, and a Mr. Haxthausen.

Mrs. Durham in 1955 recalls that at all hours of the day or night, people felt that it was their neighborly right to call her home to find out *where* the fire was.

Fraternal Hall had burned in 1912, and the Heights badly needed a meeting place or auditorium. It was proposed, therefore, to build a combination city hall and fire station on 12th and Yale on the site of the old community center. J. B. Marmion was mayor in 1914 when the cornerstone of the new imposing building was laid. That stone today is the only marker of the old Houston Heights municipality.

On March 1, 1915, Hugh Montgomery was appointed fire chief for the Heights. His new crew included: M. T. Robinson, captain; Ed. Kohlman, lieutenant; G. K. Parker, O. M. Phillips, Roy Crush, S. Lowe, and E. Hueboetter, pipemen and laddermen.

The smaller station on 18th, in the old jail building, grew as an extension of the central fire station on 12th and Yale.

PROFESSIONAL

LIFE

MEDICAL PROFESSION

The Heights *Suburbanite* on August 12, 1905 states that Dr. C. A. Wallace and Frank Johnson had bought out the Carter and Christian grocery with the purpose of continuing that business "with an experienced grocery man," W. J. Turner, in charge. But apparently the grocery store was soon changed to a pharmacy, and not too long after that change, Dr. Wallace left the Heights practice and his interest in the store. Arch Fulton then became the second partner in the business which had become known as the Nineteenth Avenue Drug Store. Later, Mr. Fulton set up Fulton's Pharmacy on the northwest corner of 19th and Ashland. However, it is the old Nineteenth Avenue Drug Store in the early development of the Heights that stands out as a landmark.

After 1906, Dr. G. J. Robinson came to the Heights and then Dr. T. A. Sinclair and Dr. B. V. Ellis. All three physicians located their offices over the drug store. These three doctors had individual offices and private practice, but always at least one "was in" and ready to help. The citizens of the north end of the Heights could depend for service at Johnson's drug store center, and the service was excellent.

49

Sometimes a patient was sent to Houston to a specialist. One lady remembers when Dr. Robinson sent her to the old Scanlan Building to Dr. John Foster "to have her tonsils taken out." That delicate attention was given at home on the dining room table. Dr. Robinson gave the anaesthetic, the child's father acted as nurse (the mother could not look at blood) and the tonsils were yanked out in good order. Most treatment was the homey sort and most patients responded without the aid of a psychiatrist.

The hotel which Carter had built as a drawing card for the de luxe character of his addition ceased operation in 1899. It was leased then to Dr. Penn B. Thornton and a Dr. Davis. No record helps to authenticate this earliest period of the hotel's conversion to a hospital, but there is evidence that these doctors did not stay with the project for any length of time. Miss Nellie Kennedy, who had been last to help with the management of the hotel, stayed on for about six months with Doctors Thornton and Davis.

In the *City Directory 1900-1901,* Houston Heights Infirmary is listed. Opposite page 89 appears a full-page advertisement by Dr. W. T. Dickey, proprietor: "Baked Alive" treatment for gout, arthritis, and most chronic diseases, and then "we cure morphine and drug habits." The benefits of the "delightfully situated" infirmary are extolled with the further inducement of "the Houston Heights car every twenty minutes." In 1902-1903, Houston Heights Hotel is back in the *Directory,* with O. M. Carter as manager. The next issue of the *Directory* omits all notice of the place, but in 1905, O. M. Carter is entered as resident at the *hotel.*

Then in 1906, came another change with "J. Alvin Horne Sanatorium" named. Dr. Horne's management did not last long, for on May 30, 1908, the Heights *Suburbanite* ran an advertisement for the Texas Christian Sanitarium and lists the following names in connection with the new management: Wm. A. Wilson, President; Dr. W. W. Lunn, Vice-President;

A. F. Sanderson, Secretary; Dr. T. A. Sinclair, House Physician. Dr. John T. Moore also had interest in the project.

Originally the building was flush with the street. At this time it was moved back for landscaping. Old pictures show the change. The new sanitarium was well kept and a park at the side and back of the building made it something of a show place. But as a hospital the converted hotel was never too great a success. After a few years the place ceased operation as the Texas Christian Sanitarium and limped out its last stage as a home for feeble-minded patients.

On June 7, 1955 the *Houston Chronicle* printed the story of the hospital's end in its column of "Forty Years Ago":

> Thirty patients are rescued as fire razes the Houston Heights Sanitarium at 345 Nineteenth. The blaze was discovered by Dr. R. E. Cloud, superintendent, shortly after noon.

Actually the fire was on June 1, 1915. The "Forty Years Ago" column was in error.

One patient proved to be the hero of the fire; he rushed upstairs and persuaded his fellow patients to play tug-of-war with him. In this way he led many to safety. But a number of the patients fled and the neighborhood spent the rest of the day trying to find them. The burning of the hotel was the "big fire" in the history of the Heights. One early resident recalls the clamor and clangor as the Houston Fire Department trucks dashed out the Boulevard from the Washington Avenue Station. Horses were still used at the time, and one great horse from that station, after the long mad run, dropped dead when he reached the scene. The building was completely destroyed.

Later, Dr. Sinclair and his associates would be the founders of a permanent hospital for the Heights, but their establishment comes after the period covered by this work as a history of Houston Heights as a municipality.

Dr. John Wroughton, after 1900, had his office and residence at 12th and Boulevard. But after 1904, Dr. Wroughton changed his office to an address on Washington Avenue. One early resident says that Dr. Wroughton was instrumental in founding the Hot Wells institution west of Houston as a health resort.

Dr. A. L. Miller also served the north section of the Heights and for a number of years after 1912 had his office above Fulton's Pharmacy. Dr. Miller is still practicing in 1955 and has his office at his home address, 13th and Yale.

In the south end of the Heights the *City Directory* in 1907 lists Dr. William Olive as physician, surgeon, and proprietor of Olive's Drug Store at 910 Yale. (It was next door to this drug store that the first volunteer fire department was housed, and above it the first Masonic Lodge in the Heights organized.) Across the street, at 909 Yale, Dr. Robert H. Towles, also listed as physician, surgeon, and proprietor of a drug store, established his practice.

There were a number of doctors living in the Heights who practiced in Houston, but in the early days there were not too many who had offices in the Heights. There is no record of a dentist practicing in the Heights. However, in the early 1900's, Dr. D. W. Whipple and his family lived between 13th and 14th on the Boulevard, and at his downtown office Dr. Whipple attended to everybody in the Heights who had the toothache.

EDUCATION

In the *City Directory 1894-1895* under "Educational" appears this entry: "Houston Heights Public School — nw cor Ashland, 20th Ave. Miss J. Deady, teacher," Very likely above a store, and certainly in a business house, education in the Heights had begun in 1893, while waiting for the erection of a school building.

Later, after 1896, when the Heights had become incorporated as a municipality, we find scattered in the minutes

52

of council meetings, data on the growing needs for adequate schools. At the meeting on December 5, 1898, John Milroy (secretary pro tem) enters an itemized account for labor amounting to $200.90 and for materials totaling $403.45 for the construction of Harvard Street School. One item, "desks — $11.00"!

Another bill for both Cooley and Harvard Schools for supplies is interesting as seen in the light of 20th century's year 1955:—

4 boxes chalk	.45
1 doz. erasers	.75
1 hand belt	.50

Altogether the year's supplies for the two schools for essential needs reached a total of $20.00. The city fathers evidently approved that last item as an expenditure of 50¢ for juvenile delinquency.

At a meeting on June 20, 1898, a motion was made by D. D. Cooley (presumably to raise the level) "that teachers of the higher grades be paid $50.00 per month and teachers of the lower grades $40.00 . . ." From the group of applicants on the list presented at the meeting, the council members proposed "election by ballot." There is no mention of referring such selection of teachers to the school board. And there was a school board at the time. However, most of the council members were also school board members. The three teachers chosen at this particular meeting were:

Miss Emerald Jones, Houston Heights
Miss Annie Thielen, Belton
Miss Lucy Clark, Hempstead

A change must have been made after the voting because the *City Directory* for the next school term (1899) does not name Miss Clark. It gives Miss Annie Thielen at Harvard and Misses Emerald M. Jones and Kate Hill at Cooley. (Miss Hill, like Miss Clark, was listed from Hempstead.)

One more note from these early records is significant of its date in the middle of winter, in January, 1899:—

Eight cords of Post Oak wood to be delivered to the several schoolhouses of the municipality at $4.00 per cord.

And on June 24, 1902, looking forward to a high school, the council deliberated an

Ordinance...to borrow $3,000 to purchase sites for schools and for the construction of school buildings.

COOLEY SCHOOL

On August 6, 1894, the Omaha and South Texas Land Company deeded to County Judge John G. Tod lots 1-6 inclusive, block 131, for $100 for public school in District 25. On 17th and Rutland, therefore, the first schoolhouse in the Heights was erected, a two-story, red brick structure with green shutters, one room downstairs and one above. This original part remains in the building today, and from the back of the building one can detect the red brick where the white surfacing has worn off.

The new building opened in 1894. D. D. Cooley was the principal speaker at the dedication ceremonies; and since it was Mr. Cooley who had led the movement to establish the school, it was suggested that it be named for him. Arthur W. Cooley remembers attending classes there with Miss J. Deady of Harrisburg as his first teacher. Miss Deady's father was honored years later when the James Deady Junior High School was named for him.

The next mention of a school in the Heights was in the *City Directory 1897-1898,* this time giving "Cooley Public School, No. 3, District 25 ws Rutland bt 16th 17th," and then in awkward fashion adding "Misses Couch, teachers." In 1899, Misses Emerald Jones and Kate Hill are named as teachers. Miss Hill continued for a number of years at Cooley; and when she resigned in the spring of 1905, on account of illness, Miss Ruby Webb finished the term. "Miss Ruby" then taught at Cooley School until her marriage in 1913 to Mr. O. F. Carroll.

While the first addition, giving the school four new rooms, was being built in 1906, classes continued over Frank

Johnson's drug store and over Kincaide Mercantile Company's store (later Lewis's grocery). Miss Lota B. Harris started teaching that year at Cooley and she followed her first grade (and evidently two or three more grades) over the Kincaide store and remained with Cooley pupils through the years. In 1939, when Miss Harris retired, she had given the Heights a lifetime of devoted, intelligent service in the teaching profession. Another teacher who for years remained at Cooley and endeared herself to the children of two generations was Miss Daisy Russell.

At first Miss Deady alone taught all eight grades. Then two teachers handled the two classrooms. After the first addition to the building, in 1906, there were six classrooms and as many teachers. At that time, too, the old red brick was painted and new white brick added to make a white building.

The Mothers Club of Cooley School was organized in 1907, the forerunner of the school's P. T. A. The mothers took turns serving hot lunches in the basement. But first they had the basement closed in from the wind and rain and had the floor cemented. Hot lunches then meant soup one day and chili the next. But the soup was a meal in itself and likewise the chili. Two slices of bread went with the bowl, and the whole dinner cost exactly 5¢. Hot dogs had not yet appeared in the history of mankind.

Mrs. D. D. Cooley served as first president of the Mothers Club. Other ladies whose names most frequently appeared in the columns of the *Suburbanite* as leaders of the club's activities were: Mesdames D. M. Duller, L. Sparks, H. J. Muller, M. Sheehan, Chas. York, J. C. Carpenter, J. W. Wilder, and J. W. Hartley.

Sometimes the mothers had teas and entertainments. One social tea and musical program was reported by the *Suburbanite* for December 12, 1908 at the home of Mrs. T. P. Griffiths. Earlier that year, on March 21, the annual spring festival featured the following program:

55

AN APRIL CANTATA

Bessie Sunshine .... Neva Robinson
Helen Heiress .... Rose Wear
Twins .... Ellen Muller
Ida Bell
Edith .... Garnett Robinson
Dora .... Marabelle Hamilton
Nell .... Cecil Hawkins
Portia .... Helen Wilson
Maud .... Abbie Mae Hartley
Kate .... Blanche Bennett
Jennie .... Mabel Jackson
School girls: Maybelle Whipple, Evelyn Burlingame, Ola
McDuff, Rose Christian, Evelyn Hombs, Leo Cushing.
A Bird in Hand .... Three Maids
"Stingy" Song in Costume .... Leo Cushing

On one memorable February 22, the ladies, each dressed as Martha Washington, celebrated George's birthday with games on the school grounds, special prizes for the children, and booths where nickels and dimes accumulated for the school's necessities. Schoolground equipment, a flag and flagpole, a piano, and classroom aids were all supplied by the Mothers Club.

HARVARD STREET SCHOOL

On September 18, 1898, Harvard School opened its doors to the children of the south end section of the Heights. At the dedication ceremonies, the members of the school board were present: D. D. Cooley, W. G. Love, Wm. A. Wilson, L. Ream, C. A. McKinney, and John A. Milroy. The *City Directory* for that year lists the school as "Houston Heights School No. 2 — cor Harvard, 8th Ave. Miss Annie M. Thielan, teacher."

The school was built on two lots at Harvard and 8th, and its name derived from its location, although later the word *Street* was dropped from its title.

Before the building could be erected, it was necessary to secure the enrollment of at least thirty pupils. Interested mothers accomplished this feat, and a one-room building followed fast. There were fifty desks and thirty pupils in the first five grades, with Miss Thielen as teacher of all classes. In 1900, Miss Thielen was transferred to Cooley School and replaced at Harvard by her sister, Miss Alice Thielen.

In 1902, rooms were added to the building and three teachers then employed: Misses Yeager, Ayleen Sharp, and Lucille Schindler. This enlarged, three-room frame building was still serving in 1911 when a view book of the Heights printed a picture of the first brick unit beside the old building.

Besides the Misses Thielen, a number of early teachers served at Harvard through the years and should be mentioned in a history of that school: Misses Florence Keene, Vera Harris (before Miss Harris transferred to the High School) Miss Nanno Maynard and Marie W. Finney. Later, W. H. Elrod served as principal, after the school had grown into an impressive center of learning. Mr. Elrod's term at Harvard expired with the amalgamation of the Heights into the Houston Public School system.

In 1910, the Mothers Club of Harvard School was organized. Mr. and Mrs. J. M. Limbocker (who owned and edited the *Suburbanite*) sponsored an all-day picnic on their spacious lawn, across from the old Heights Natatorium, to raise funds for the club's work. Mrs. Limbocker's niece, Mrs. D. D. Smeaton, was the first president of the Mothers Club. Other outstanding members were: Mesdames H. C. Colley, P. M. Granberry, L. E. Van Valkenburgh, and C. C. Young.

Harry Van Demark was a rising young playwright of the Heights at the time, and he staged a production for funds to fill in the school grounds. An old newspaper clipping remarks that the "school board was persuaded to repair the roof."

In general the needs of the school fell upon the shoulders of the people of the neighborhood. In 1911, like the mothers of the children at Cooley, the mothers at Harvard School were preparing soup and chili for hot lunches. The growth of the school system in the Heights was not left to the school board and the teachers, except in matters of classroom procedure. An active interest in the welfare of their children is apparent in all records of the people of the Heights and extended to tangible evidence in getting things done.

HOUSTON HEIGHTS HIGH SCHOOL

On the site of the present Milroy Park, on the northwest corner of Yale and 12th, the first Heights High School was erected in 1904. The property was purchased from D. W. Whipple, "Acknowledged 19 April, 1904 – Deed Records of Harris County." According to deed records and to information in the minutes of the Heights Council, there is no longer doubt about the fact that all school property in the Heights was purchased by the people.

A. Hugh Russell was the first principal of the new high school, and the faculty included: Misses Ilse Frischmeyer, Minnie M. Gillespie, C. Ethel Bagby, Margaret Guthrie, Mary G. Smither, and Ima Cully. These names are listed in the *City Directory, 1905-1906* which would indicate that the school was in operation the preceding year. No more definite date can be set since all records were later lost when the building burned.

The *Suburbanite* has notice of the high school graduation exercises on June 17, 1905, and states that "Miss Lottie Burlingame has the honor of being the first graduate of our high school." The next year on June 2, 1906, the paper again lists graduation and names those receiving diplomas: Neva Robinson, Mattie Jackson, Ralph Cooley, Floyd Shelby Sisk, and Phillip Patella. The third class, finishing in 1907, included: Sophia Borgstrom, Yandell Coombs, Annie Price, Georgia Peck, Helen Milroy, and Clifton Wilson.

The building later, and evidently at first, served to accommodate the overflow of elementary pupils from Cooley and Harvard. In fact, for many years the downstairs rooms of the two-story high school building had grammar grades only. In that period, the average elementary pupil did not go on to high school. No wonder the high school graduate then could "read and write," since only the gifted student persevered and was thought worthy of an education. The number of high school pupils was not in proportion to the community's number of elementary grade students.

A. H. Russell after his first term as principal and superintendent, left the Heights. S. H. Hickman is listed as his successor for the school term 1906-1907. The following year Mr. Russell returned as superintendent and served in that capacity until the spring of 1911 when he resigned. Lawson W. Greathouse served as principal of the high school during Mr. Russell's term of office as superintendent. Then in 1912, M. L. Donner is given in the *Directory* as principal. Miss Nellie S. Ferguson was "acting principal" in 1913, followed by W. C. Wahlers. Mr. Greathouse had succeeded Mr. Russell as superintendent.

No *City Directory* was printed in 1916, but in 1917, S. P. Waltrip for the first time appears in the *Directory* as superintendent, with I. V. Brock as principal. After that date high school progress is noticeable. This does not mean that those who went before made little progress, but rather that the necessity of high school education for "all pupils" had all over the country become the accepted norm. And preparations were being made to meet the demand.

Also, in 1918 the Heights joined the City of Houston, and the Houston Independent School District already had junior high schools.* The *City Directory 1920-1921* lists what might have become a fact during the preceding year, the existence of

Houston Heights Senior High School...Blvd cor w 20th
S. P. Waltrip prin.

* Here this work is under necessity to deviate from its first purpose to cover the history of the Heights only until annexation.

and another entry

Houston Heights Junior High School ... Yale nw cor 12th

At last the Houston Heights High School was housed in a building taken over exclusively for high school work, on the site of the old Heights Playground; and a junior high school was established as preparatory for senior high school courses.

Then came the upset; the building at 12th and Yale burned on March 13, 1924. Since there was already a junior high school nearer the city and serving the people between Houston and the Heights, it was decided to make the high school on 20th into a junior high school for the northwest section and find a location nearer to the more populated district needing a senior high school. The site chosen was the block between Arlington and Oxford and between 13th and 14th.

More definite names were also desired and the junior high school became Alexander Hamilton, while the new senior high was called John H. Reagan.

Serving longest at the Heights High School and moving on to Reagan were Miss Vera Harris, who had earlier taught at Harvard and who was a sister to Miss Lota Harris of Cooley, and Miss Nellie Ferguson. Miss Ferguson continued in the system until 1954 and died in December of that year. Miss Vera Harris retired with her sister in 1939 and moved to Austin. Miss Hope Finfrock is another name now cherished by the many pupils that she taught at Heights High School. Miss Finfrock's father, P. H. Finfrock, taught in the Houston Public Schools for 29 years, and his family was outstanding in the academic circles of the Heights.

A high standard was maintained from the beginning at the Heights High School. To its teachers in particular the people of the Heights owe a debt of deep gratitude for the inculcation of sound principles that have marked the development of Heights history.

60

COLORED SCHOOLS

The first school for colored children in the Heights was opened in 1902, on 23rd, west of Nashua, with Miss Mary McKinney as teacher. The weekly *Suburbanite* on August 18, 1906, notices a new building there in that year:

> The Newbanks Brothers have just finished a new school house for the colored children on Twenty-third west of Nashua St. It is 24 by 40 ft., 13 ft. ceilings, well finished, and painted white.

The Deed Records of Harris County (vol. 199, pp. 580-581) show "Houston Heights Municipality to O. M. Carter property in exchange for a lot between 7th and 8th on Railroad, dated November 6, 1906." In 1907, a school for the Colored children in the south end of the Heights was built on that lot. It was called the Eighth Avenue School and was located on West 8th and Railroad, with Miss Jennie D. Smith as teacher. In 1908, this school is listed at 725 Waverly, and the following year at 727 Waverly, where it has remained permanently located.

In 1910, the Twenty-third Avenue School had two teachers: Misses Virginia Cornish and Virginia L. Nelson. In 1918, before annexation, the school on Waverly had three teachers and the one on 23rd two teachers.

CHURCHES

The William Peacocks were living in the Heights in 1893, and Mrs. Peacock says that the first religious services that she recalls were non-denominational. The congregation was termed the Union Sunday School (specifically named as un-attached to any church) and met in an unfinished house on 16th and Boulevard. This organization then moved its place of worship to Cooley School and for many years C. A. McKinney was its superintendent.

Finally on February 10, 1906, the *Suburbanite* announced that the "Union Sunday School, which had been organized through the persistent efforts of Mrs. W. C. McBride," is closing "now that the different churches have Sunday

Schools" so that the "attendants might go the church school of their choice."

The *City Directory* lists St. Stephens Episcopal Mission in the 1895-1896 yearbook, while the rector, the Rev. Benjamin A. Rogers, still resided at 609 Elgin. The mission was located at the Cooley School building. After 1896 each year until 1903 the Rogers family is given at 1316 Boulevard and the mission still at Cooley School. In 1904, the Rev. Rogers died, and before that date, in 1903, the mission had been dropped from the *Directory*. The Rogers family remained for a number of years in the family home.

The early organization of the Episcopalian congregation makes that denomination first in the history of church services in the Heights. However, this congregation erected no building, and St. Andrews Episcopal Church, which was organized a number of years later, could hardly be said to have been a continuation of this first mission.

This brief history then will take up a short sketch of only the very first churches that continued without interruption and which built permanent church plants.

FIRST PRESBYTERIAN CHURCH

C. A. McKinney, besides serving as superintendent with the Union Sunday School, also served in the same capacity for the First Presbyterian Church. This congregation first met on July 19, 1903, in Harvard Street Schoolhouse. After a few years, services were held in the hall of the building that later became known as the Nineteenth Avenue Drug Store. The Rev. H. F. Olmstead served as first pastor and in 1905 was succeeded by Rev. R. D. Wear. In 1906, the congregation completed the first brick church building in the Heights, on the corner of 18th and Rutland.

People of all denominations loved Brother Wear. He lived near the Dexter home on West 17th, and boarding with the Wear family was Dr. Guff J. Robinson. One of the early social events in the Heights was Dr. Robinson's wedding to Miss Neva Robinson, performed by Rev. Wear, in the Presbyterian Church.

62

COLLINS MEMORIAL CHURCH

In the spring of 1903, the first Methodist Episcopal Church of Houston Heights was organized. The early meetings were held in Harvard Street School. The Rev. M. D. Collins was pastor and personally attended to the construction of the first church, a frame building on the east side of Harvard between 9th and 10th. Rev. Collins died before the building was completed and his funeral was the first service held in the church. He had endeared himself to his people and his early death was deeply felt. Later, the congregation decided to name their church in his honor. The building that Rev. Collins erected is now called Fellowship Hall.

Another building was erected in 1915, which is now called Schrode Hall in honor of Rev. T. J. Schrode, who was then pastor. Rev. Schrode raised funds for the new building by the "Joash Chest." He gave each member of the congregation a dollar to invest and return with the increase for the church fund.

In 1926, both Fellowship Hall and Schrode Hall were moved to the present location of the church on 11th and Harvard, where an imposing church plant has kept pace with the rapid growth of the church membership.

The early pastors were: Rev. M. D. Collins, 1903; Rev. Edward W. Osburn, 1903-1906; Rev. Whitford, part of 1907; Rev. Wm. H. Donner, 1907-1910; Rev. C. L. Elliott, 1910-1912; Rev. H. H. McCain, 1912-1914; Rev. T. J. Schrode, 1914-1917; Rev. C. W. Rogers, 1917-1919.

FIRST BAPTIST

The First Baptist Church of Houston Heights was organized in March, 1904, and the following summer purchased a tent and held regular services on the corner of 9th and Yale. Rev. E. D. Hamilton was first pastor.

In January, 1905, the tent burned and the church rented a three-room house in the 200 block on West Ninth, until it could complete its new building at 919 Yale Street. By 1917 more spacious grounds were necessary for expansion, and the Yale Street property was sold. Services were then held in the High School building until after annexation, when a permanent location would be made on 9th and Harvard.

GRACE METHODIST CHURCH

Grace Methodist Church was organized by a handful of members in the fall of 1905, and at first was known as Methodist Episcopal Church, South, of Houston Heights. Rev. S. S. McKenney was appointed first pastor. J. D. Freeman served as Chairman of the Board of Stewards; C. A. McKinney was again listed as Sunday School Superintendent; Mrs. George Zimmer acted as President of the Women's Missionary Society.

At first there was no building and the members met for worship at the Harvard Street School, but it was not long before a frame building was erected on the corner of 13th and Yale. In 1912, the first brick unit of the present group of church buildings was completed.

ALL SAINTS CATHOLIC CHURCH

All Saints Catholic Church was organized early in 1908 when the Most Rev. N. A. Gallagher, Bishop of Galveston, commissioned Father G. T. Walsh to start a parish in the Heights. Permission was obtained to say Mass in Fraternal Hall. Father Walsh resided in Galveston and came to Houston on Sundays. Meetings of the church committee were held after Mass.

Immediately four lots were purchased on 10th and Harvard, and in 1909 the white brick church was completed. The first church was located where the school building is at the present time. In 1912, the priest's residence was built on the corner, where the present church is located. No school was built until 1913, and then only a three-room frame structure was erected. The Dominican Sisters had taught catechism from the beginning; and when the school was opened, they had charge.

The greatest asset of the new parish was the kindly nature of its first pastor. Father Walsh had all the qualities that endear a priest to his people, and furthermore he understood the hardships involved in building a new parish. The Heights was sincerely sorry when All Saints lost Father Walsh in 1914 to Annunciation Church. He was succeeded by Father John Gallagher.

BAPTIST TEMPLE

In May, 1908, Judge T. M. Kennerly started organizing Baptist Temple for members of his faith who lived in the north end of the Heights. This church was organized June 14, 1908, with 19 charter members. Services were held over Lewis's grocery store on West 19th and a library was begun at the same location.

A scholarly German minister, the Rev. Fred Huhns, was the first pastor and served until 1910. Rev. Huhns was also the founder of the Baptist Temple Library, and in this capacity served people of all faiths in that end of the Heights. Rev. Evander Ammons served after 1910 until 1915 and was followed by Rev. E. P. West, who remained until after annexation.

In 1911, a new brick building was begun on 20th and Rutland, on land donated by O. M. Carter, and was completed in 1912. This structure formed the first unit of Baptist Temple's present impressive church plant.

FIRST LIBRARY IN THE HEIGHTS

Although Baptist Temple was not the first Baptist Church in the Heights, entitling it to a place in the history of "firsts," it still had the unique distinction of starting the Heights' first library venture.

Rev. F. Huhns interested people of all denominations in the need for a reading room and library. He held services over Lewis's store on 19th and Ashland and partitioned off the back of the room for his library.

Children could get anything there, from *Anne of Green Gables* to a popular series of the period called *The Dorothy Dainty Books* (a somewhat milder dose of the *Little Colonel* series). *Toby Tyler, Mrs. Wiggs,* they were all to be had at the Baptist Temple Library. And since the whole community supported the library, the books were available to all. Besides, Rev. Huhns was a gentle person, peculiarly suited to remind the reader of Charles Lamb or the author of *Alice in Wonderland.*

On June 29, 1909, the library was formally opened and Miss Julia Ideson was the principal speaker. Miss Julia Spencer and Miss Agnes Jeter had charge of the library, and Judge T. M. Kennerly was its chief sponsor and its guiding spirit. Not only with the activities of the Baptist Church but with the civic development of old Houston Heights, Judge Kennerly stood out as a pioneer leader. Rev. Huhns was an intellectual and his zeal to establish the library was matched only by Judge Kennerly's help in its organization.

After 1912, when the Baptist Temple had built a church on West 20th, the library continued to function, but principally then as a denominational unit.

There is no record of any other library facilities for the general public in the Heights before annexation.

NEWSPAPERS

According to the *City Directory 1903-1904* the *Houston Heights News* was issued semi-weekly. Lester L. Allen is given as editor and proprietor. Evidently a short-lived project, this publication seems to have left no other record.

Since the *Suburbanite* issued its first number on January 28, 1905, there seems reason to believe that possibly this new journal took over the printing press and equipment of the earlier *Houston Heights News.* At least the *Suburbanite* followed fast after the first newspaper, but it lasted long and remained a vital force in the life of old Houston Heights.

Across the street from the Vieweger home, on 3rd and Harvard, lived Mr. and Mrs. J. M. Limbocker, who after 1904 owned and edited the Heights newspaper. Their *Suburbanite* was a weekly publication and a reliable source of information. Everybody in the Heights subscribed.

All local happenings usually got into the paper on page one. If a special issue used up that page for a display of pictures or the promotion of some new improvement, then local news found space elsewhere. But almost always six of the other seven pages were devoted to serials and feature stories, probably syndicated material now referred to in newspaper parlance as "canned stuff." The eighth page ordinarily ran items of interest of Channeyville (where Heights Boulevard merges into the Washington Avenue area), Vick's Park (north end of Waugh Drive, today cutting into the old Channeyville district), Brunner (farther west of Channeyville and bordering the Heights on the southwest), and also Harrisburg. Why the *Suburbanite* of the Heights printed news of Harrisburg, on the other side of Houston, is not clear.

It is the page that ran "Heights Local News" that today makes the *Suburbanite* important. This weekly chronicle of life in the Heights kept a fifteen years account of Heights history which ended only with the life of the publication on February 6, 1920. Residents moving in were announced. Marriages, births, and deaths are all there. One odd feature in the early years of this newspaper pertained to the post office: separate lists of the names of gentlemen and of ladies who had failed to call for mail were printed. School history and elections got space. Even the court proceedings (and the fancy fines) in the *Suburbanite* trace the picture of Houston Heights.

Besides helping with the newspaper, Mrs. Limbocker was also active in the social life of the Heights, and her husband, known as Judge Limbocker, served long on different civic boards and committees. Later, Mrs. D. D. Smeaton, Mrs. Limbocker's niece, lived in the old home.

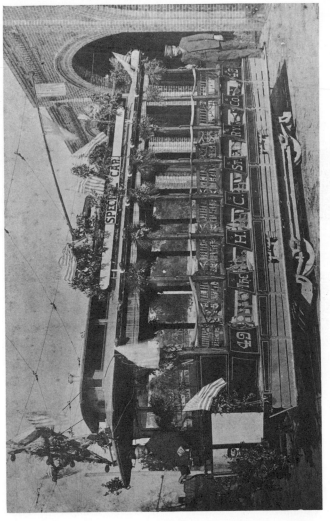

EARLY STREET CAR TO THE HEIGHTS

This picture belonged to Mr. C. A. McKinney, who was in charge of Mr. Carter's street car interests. This car was No. 49 of the Houston City Street Railway Company, and it is believed that it was decorated for the first run to the Heights.

Street car service made possible the opening up of the new addition to Houston.

HEIGHTS BOULEVARD

This residence at 1530 Boulevard at the time this picture was taken was the home of the H. A. Paine family.

THE PLANING MILL

The Electric Company's two-story building is shown north of the Planing Mill and across the street from the Electric Company was the Furniture Factory that lasted longest and was best known to old Houston Heights as the Pickle Factory. The street car ran out on the railroad tracks to this business section.

TEXAS CHRISTIAN SANITARIUM,
19th and Ashland Streets

In 1908, the old hotel became the Texas Christian Sanitarium. Dr. T. A. Sinclair was the House Physician. Later, Dr. Sinclair would found the Heights Hospital.

"I was glad when they said unto me, let us go into the House of the Lord."

St. Stephens Episcopal Mission,

Houston Heights, Texas.

Rev. B. A. Rogers,

Minister.

Regular Church Services at the Cooley School House first
and third Sundays in each month at 11 A. M. ● ● ● ●
Union Sunday School every Sunday morning at 10 o'clock.

You and your family and friends are most cordially invit-
ed and urged to attend these services.

Have not you a duty to perform in this direction?

The Church is the bulwark of society.

Religious services should be maintained in every community.

"Enter into his gates with thanksgiving and into his courts
with praise."

YOU WILL BE WELCOME.

The non-denominational Union Sunday School here listed was the
first religious organization in the Heights.

St. Stephens Episcopal Mission was the first Church organization
established.

FIRST PRESBYTERIAN CHURCH, 18th and Rutland Streets

FIRST M. E. CHURCH, between 9th and 10th on Harvard

ALL SAINTS CATHOLIC CHURCH, 10th and Harvard Streets

GRACE METHODIST CHURCH, 13th Avenue and Yale Street

FIRST BAPTIST CHURCH, 919 Yale Street

BAPTIST TEMPLE, 20th Avenue and Rutland Street

HARVARD STREET SCHOOL, 8th and Harvard Streets

COOLEY SCHOOL, 17th and Rutland Street

76

HOUSTON HEIGHTS HIGH SCHOOL, 12th and Yale Streets

HOUSTON HEIGHTS WATER AND LIGHT COMPANY'S PARK

D. D. COOLEY'S RESIDENCE, 18th and Boulevard

JOHN A. MILROY'S RESIDENCE, 11th and Boulevard

This home at 1530 Boulevard was built for Col. N. L. Mills. From 1894 until 1901 it was the home of the Nelson A. Baker family and then until 1908 the H. A. Paine family resided here. After 1908 for about 30 years it was the W. A. McNeill residence.

This home at 1316 Boulevard was built for William Shannon. Later it was the residence of Rev. B. A. Rogers and often called the Tempest home because Mrs. Tempest, the widowed daughter of the Rogers family, also lived here. After 1920 it became known as the Carter home when O. M. Carter made it his residence.

EARLY STORES

The A. J. Myers Store opened on August 12, 1902, on the southeast corner of 9th and Yale and for years covered the entire territory of the Heights in its delivery service.

In 1912, Dave Kaplan leased the F. F. Ibsch Store on 22nd and Yale. Two years later Kaplan built his own store across from Ibsch. Kaplan's and Ben Hur thus has a record of 44 years of continuous service in the Heights.

Houston Heights Volunteer Fire Department, organized September 1, 1908. Horace C. Olive, Fire Chief, holding reins in picture.

The 19th Avenue Drug Store, corner of 19th and Ashland.

At the Heights Playground, children lining up for the Carnival sponsored by the Woman's Club in 1912 for the benefit of the new Club House.

EARLY LEADERS

C. A. McKINNEY

D. D. COOLEY

JOHN A. MILROY

T. M. KENNERLY

MAYORS

W. G. LOVE

D. BARKER

R. F. ISBELL

J. B. MARMION

John A. Milroy (see preceding page) was also Mayor.

Mrs. Enger Moller, early resident of 1897 selected by her community as the "Queen of Yesterday" for the Heights' 50th Anniversary in 1941.

Mrs. Hortense Ward, who with her husband, Judge W. H. Ward, founded the Law Firm of Ward and Ward.

Mrs. Irene McBride, prominent early settler and first postmaster of the Heights.

Mrs. Fred F. Dexter, social leader who helped to organize early clubs in the Heights.

HOUSTON HEIGHTS FOOTBALL TEAM, 1907

Back row: Arch Fulton, Denton Cooley, Carl Van Liew, Boyd Neubanks, Coach.

Middle row: Harvey Maack, Fred Sparks, Gus Maack, Unidentified player, Big Boy Barnes.

Front row: Babe White, Wade Sheehan, Harry Sheehan, Captain, Frank Williams, Otis Paine.

Third Graduating Class (1907) of Houston Heights High School.

Back row: Sophia Borgstrom, Yandell Coombs, Annie Price, Georgia Peck.

Front row: Helen Milroy, Clifton Wilson.

A group of Sunshine Society members celebrating the 80th birthday of Mrs. Bacon at the home of her daughter, Mrs. C. A. McKinney.

Back row: Mesdames E. M. Johnston, C. A. McKinney, F. C. Van Liew, T. A. Sinclair, M. Sheehan.

Front row: Mesdames S. D. Wilkins, P. O. Endt, Cynthia A. Bacon, R. J. Webb.

THE MANDOLIN CLUB

The Mandolin Club was organized in 1916 by Mrs. Eugene Cook. Mr. A. M. Krueger, musician and florist, made and patented the lyralin in this picture, taken at the Herman T. Keller home at 1448 Boulevard.

Left to right, back row: Marian Burge, Mrs. G. J. Robinson, Mrs. E. V. Whitty, Mrs. Carrie Lafiew Pease, Mrs. Eugene Cooke, Mrs. Jackson, Mrs. C. E. Oliver, Mrs. Everts, Mrs. Nellie Overstreet, Ruth Taylor.

Front row: Mae Hawkins, Garnett Robinson, Edna Scott.

Mrs. Myrtle Cook Lowry   Miss Amine Welling

HOUSTON HEIGHTS MUSIC CLUB

Members

Mesdames

C. E. Oliver	E. A. Cook
Myrtle Cook Lowry	J. E. Johnson
J. W. Wilder	E. J. Hill
E. Ammons	M. C. Lane
G. J. Robinson	J. M. Bender
G. McLeod	C. C. Beavens
C. C. Young	Alex Peddie
T. P. Griffiths	W. W. Kellogg
Florence Barziza	C. C. Wenzel

Misses

Hazel Hawkins	Louise Florence
Mabelle Poutra	Elsie Vieweger
Blanche Bennett	Clementine Risley
Emily Beavens	Florence Youssi
Amine Welling	Althea Lane

Mrs. C. E. Oliver, President

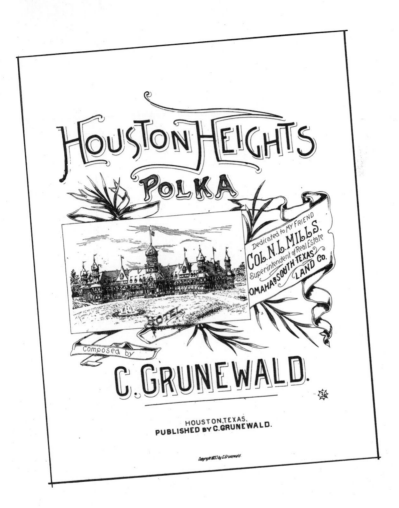

HOUSTON HEIGHTS POLKA

Mrs. D. D. Cooley   Mrs. W. A. Renn

Woman's Club House, 1846 Harvard Street. The
ground for this building was given by Mr. and Mrs.
D. D. Cooley. Mrs. W. A. Renn, President of the
Club, presided at the reception which marked the
opening of the building on Friday, October 18, 1912.

Anna Zagst	Catherine Cox Blackburn	Lucia Sellers	Mae Hawkins
Thelma Freet	Agnes Jeter	Josephine Wilcox	Hattie Stone Browning
Marabell Hamilton	Maree Shaffer	Esther Dyke	Christine Freeman Carter
Marjorie Lappine Adams	Garnett Robinson	Cecil Hawkins	Nina Parrish

Belle Williamson

The earliest picture that could be found of

THE NEAUBEAUX CLUB

about 1920

The Camp

Houston Heights

Bridging White Oak Bayou.

Beginning to Grade
The Boulevard

The Clearing at the Ravine
West Boulevard

Sanders Eng. Co.
St Louis.

OPENING UP THE HEIGHTS – An illustration from *HOUSTON ILLUSTRATED, A FEW FACTS*, 1893.

Another page from *HOUSTON ILLUSTRATED, A FEW FACTS,* 1893.

93

SOCIAL
LIFE

COOMBS PARK OR FOREST PARK

On March 19, 1873, the Texas Constitution was amended to aid railroad construction by grants of land allowing 20 sections to the mile of railroad provided. The International-Great-Northern was one of the roads affected by this encouragement. Opening up Texas by providing transportation facilities was a stimulus to immigration. It was around this time that a young man from Hartford, Kentucky, Eden L. Coombs, came to Houston to work as a teamster boss for the I. & G. N. Railroad.

In this work he met J. J. Sweeney, and in 1881 the two men formed a partnership in the Sweeney-Coombs Jewelry Company. Later engaged in real estate investments, they acquired the Sweeney-Coombs Opera House. Opened on November 3, 1890 by Graus Opera Company in *The Gondoliers,* this opera house was Houston's principal theater.

Undoubtedly Coombs in the theater business became acquainted with the entertainment world. Also he became acquainted with Mr. Carter and Mr. Cooley, who around 1890, were organizing the Omaha and South Texas Land Company to assimilate a variety of interests. So why not an amusement park?

A recorded deed filed January 17, 1894, states that on December 19, 1893, D. D. Cooley, acting as trustee for the Omaha and South Texas Land Company

> had transferred to E. L. Coombs for $1,500.00 all of lots...
> of block...which amounted to all that portion of blocks
> 318, 319 lying north of White Oak Bayou including all
> intervening streets and alleys south of but not including
> Fourth Avenue.

There were later entries for more property, for further consideration, to E. L. Coombs and wife, Julia Coombs. In all, the Coombs acquired 64 acres, from 208 south of 2nd to 4th, with the bayou in the middle of the property. On the northeast side of the bayou, Coombs planned his park, which came to be known as Coombs Park or Forest Park.

On the east side of 3rd and Boulevard, he dug a lake, large and deep. Here he had trick high-diving, made more interesting by the presence of alligators in the water.

At the end of Harvard, on the banks of the bayou, he built a natatorium. A view book of Houston, *Houston Illustrated, a Few Facts,* gives a picture of the building surrounding the pool. Coombs built in the flamboyant style of Coney Island's heyday. The picture shows a pleasure pier, two and a half stories, with dressing rooms for each floor, like galleries around the pool. The impressive building was topped off with one large round tower and two smaller turrets, each waving a flag. The building later burned and a more modest structure was erected.

Sunday afternoon was the park's big day. At three o'clock every Sunday, a Mrs. Roaming (significant name) went up in a balloon, with a monkey for a companion. Sometimes the monkey went up alone. The balloon had a basket and when the lady got ready to come down, she pulled a valve and gradually as the gas escaped, the balloon descended. When the monkey went up alone, the valve was *fixed* so that the gas was gradually leaking before the ascension.

There was a track in the park for goat racing, and the children brought their pets, harnassed to various little wagons or traps, and took part in the race for prizes. Mr. Coombs also provided a zoo with all kinds of animals for the special delight of the children. Between his home and the bayou, extending back to Yale Street, he had an ostrich farm and children of the Heights loved to go near the fence to see the birds. These, too, were for the park.

On the southeast side of the bayou, where the lots were high above the street, Mr. Coombs built a fine old house of the type of big, white sprawling mansions popular around 1900. As homes filled in the lots nearby, the elevated section became known as "Coombs Terrace."

THE NATATORIUM LASTED

The Coombs Park represented a big investment and covered a big tract of land. Mr. Coombs died early in 1900 and gradually the property was sold as lots. The abstract for the property on which the natatorium was built shows transfer to P. M. Granberry, the William Marsh Rice Estate, T. J. Harper, and finally in 1907 to Max Vieweger. It was the Vieweger family that ran the Heights natatorium for its longest, most successful period. For many years it was operated by Dr. W. H. Eaton, husband of Olga Vieweger. C. H. Dean was the last owner of the old Heights nat. Mr. Dean tells that he stopped operation in 1927, that he lost the property in the depression and then bought it back again. Today the old nat is filled in. For years it was a drawing card to the Heights before "swimming pools" existed; now it is a vacant lot with no indication of a former state of life filled with fun and laughter.

CAMP TOM BALL

Recruits for the Spanish-American War were trained in a tent encampment, Camp Tom Ball, on the east side of the Boulevard, extending along Coombs' property and making the corner of 4th and Boulevard the General Headquarters. Mrs. P. V. Meyers (formerly Yandell Coombs) remembers that three officers and their wives asked for rooms with the Coombs family and lived in her home at that time. The

Company was the Fourth Texas Regiment, and the first troops to arrive were the Smith County Rifles.

The Ladies Military Aid Society met the national emergency by making clothes and surgical d r e s s i n g s for the soldiers. On August 12, 1898, a preliminary protocol was signed which practically ended the war, and on September 28 the troops in the Heights broke camp.

FRATERNAL HALL

The Deed Records of Harris County show that "The Fraternal Hall Association of Houston Heights, Texas" had b o u g h t lots 13, 14, and 15 in Block 186 for $850.00 on December 8, 1905.

The *Houston Post* on June 29, 1906, states that "The Odd Fellows of Houston Heights have taken steps to erect a combination hall and auditorium on a lot recently purchased on Yale Street near the High School Building...(for) lodge purposes and...an a u d i t o r i u m where all kinds of public gatherings or theatrical performances can be held. The Knights of Pythias...will o c c u p y the lodge room also..."

There is a seeming confusion here about who owned the lots and who was building. Evidently the Fraternal Hall Association e x i s t e d within the Odd Fellows Lodge and possibly within the Knights of Pythias, or was attached to those organizations.

Records show that the Association borrowed $5,000 from W. L. Thompson, a member of the Odd Fellows Lodge; and the building was erected at 1204 Yale Street. However, financial trouble set in, and on August 22, 1911, a deed on record in Harris County Court House states that the Fraternal Hall Association conveyed all title and interests in real estate, improvements, furniture, and fixtures to W. L. Thompson "in full satisfaction of indebtedness of corporation." The deed was e x e c u t e d by C. A. Mc K i n n e y, president, and R. H. Towles, secretary, of the Fraternal Hall A s s o c i a t i o n of Houston Heights, and agreed to by

Houston Heights Lodge No. 225, I. O. O. F., and Houston Heights Knights of Pythias, No. 269.

The stockholders of the Fraternal Hall Association at the time of "sale" of property to W. L. Thompson, on August 22, 1911, were listed as follows:

G. W. Wilson	D. B. Henrichs	G. W. Hawkins
R. E. Turrentine	Geo. A. Hart	P. V. Wyatt
W. D. Bradshaw	Paul Roffall	O. P. Woodburn
A. J. Myers	C. A. McKinney	Jno. A. Milroy
W. G. Love	J. L. Durham	D. Barker
W. L. Thompson	D. D. Cooley	T. V. West
R. H. Towles	J. W. Foote	Fred F. Dexter
J. W. Hartley	D. D. Smeaton	W. T. Pankey
Chas. Horn	H. Henrichsen	M. J. Shlem
Ben Reinecke	C. E. Oliver	

Apart from the data connected with its building, Fraternal Hall to the average old-timer recalls many happy memories. The building was ready for occupancy by 1907, and in it all kinds of meetings, civic entertainments, and local shows had cover. Some of the shows were unusually good. *Mrs. Temple's Telegram,* starring Mrs. Myrtle Cook Lowry, with Mrs. W. G. Love, and Dr. H. K. Hodes in the supporting cast, drew a big house. Mrs. Myrtle Cook Lowry directed most of the plays. Later, Mrs. Lowry moved from the Heights and became associated with radio production in Chicago. In the early days in the Heights, Fred Minster, Harry Van Demark, E. V. Whitty, Hugh Royall and Dr. Hodes gave professional skill to many amateur performances.* Harry Van Demark was making a name for himself as a rising playwright and he was especially active at Fraternal Hall.

At that time, the New York plays regularly toured the country and Houston saw the best of Broadway at the old Sweeney-Coombs Opera House, and then at the same place when it was called the Prince Theater, so that home talent

---

*Heights citizens are justly proud of Dr. Hodes' son, General Henry (Hank) Hodes, who in 1956 was appointed commanding officer of all American troops in Germany.

was not easily over-estimated. Of course, Fraternal Hall served many purposes, and not all entertainment was even intended to meet professional standards. That was the age when little girls "took elocution" and even at birthday parties they were asked "to recite." Older girls gave dramatic monologues, sometimes musical monologues. One piece that was rendered so often most audiences knew it by heart was "Speak up, Ike, and Spress Yourself." Terpsichorean art then took the place of tap dancing today.

At Fraternal Hall, the promising young pianist would cross her hands with great grace of movement as she gave "Over the Waves" what was indicated as "variations." One young team of enthusiasts regularly rendered an old favorite called "S T I --- N G Y" which song ended with gestures indicating that *stingy* "means you." Something like the old song of the same period that everybody was singing, "H a double r i, g a n --- that's me." Of course, "Harrigan" doesn't mean a thing unless you remember that everybody was singing it. But whether the entertainment was good or merely insipid, everybody enjoyed those programs, and the Heights was shocked when Fraternal Hall burned in 1912.

Then for a time the upper floor in Whiteside's Hall was used for entertainments, but that building also burned in 1912. One unusually good play produced at Whiteside's auditorium was *David Garrick* with E. V. Whitty in the lead.

HEIGHTS PLAYGROUND

There was no free amusement park for children until May 22, 1909, when the Heights Playground was opened at the end of the boulevard on 20th. The property had been offered to All Saints Catholic Church, but the church committee had decided that a more central location was desirable. Mr. Carter then donated the lots for a playground. It was not a large park, but it did provide swings and on certain nights in the summer gave free movies, usually movies too old to show in the theaters. Mabel Norman and Blanche Sweet in clothes that were already long out of style provided laughs for the crowd. And, of course, Charlie Chaplin was also in the playground movies. Movement was particularly funny in those old silent films because walking (in general, not just in comic pictures) was rapid and jerky.

Churches and organizations had socials in the park and the whole community turned out. This playground disappeared when the school building at the end of the Boulevard on 20th took in the park property.

POPULAR ROADS IN THE HEIGHTS

Twentieth Street in front of the playground ran east as a shell road through a stretch of country with almost no houses, only Spencer's Dairy at the bend where the road turned south, and on Shearn Street it ran into Houston Avenue. Everybody who had a horse and buggy came into Houston that way when they had plenty of time to jog along, or when they wanted a quiet road where the horse would hardly run into one of those automobiles that were making horses *shy*.

Another favorite for buggy riding was the Yale Street Road. There were a few truck farms out that way and beautiful country, fine for hunting and berry picking, although there were many signs on fences that read POSTED — KEEP OUT.

The third popular road was the old Shepherd Drive. Just before the automobile became common, J. W. Link built a home on Montrose Boulevard that was said to have gold doorknobs. Few of the visitors outside the home could really get close enough to test the story for themselves. But going down Shepherd for several miles with only an odd farmhouse here and there along the route, the Heights family could drive on a Sunday afternoon and finally skirt around the famous Link home to wonder at its splendor at journey's end. The drive in the country was delightful. Today the University of St. Thomas occupies the old Link home and there is no gold in sight.

There was also a nice drive across Washington Avenue and on, a short distance to Vick's Park and Lake. Here, not fenced off, was a property where visitors were allowed to picnic in beautiful rolling country around a good sized lake. The big white house on the bluff was the Vick family's home, and only there did visitors hesitate to intrude. Now the lake is drained and engineers, in the sunken-garden effect thus created, have worked out Houston's most intricate pattern of intersecting traffic lanes. Heights people now pass *through* Vick's Lake in Waugh Drive's celebrated Clover Leaf.

HORSE AND BUGGY THEN THE AUTOMOBILE

Before the advent of the automobile, the Heights had a livery stable, and at home many families kept a horse and buggy, and maybe a surrey. The Roffall family lived in the Heights and Mr. Roffall operated one of the largest carriage factories in Houston. Bradshaw Feed Company did a big business selling to citizens who owned either a cow or a horse, or both. Bradshaw's was located on 19th and Railroad, opposite the waterworks.

And then came the automobile! The *Suburbanite* in this instance heralded the occasion. For September 9, 1905, came this announcement:

AFTERNOON TEA

Mrs. Geo. Hawkins, president of the ladies' society of the M. E. Church, assisted by Mrs. J. M. Limbocker, will give a tea next Tuesday afternoon from 3 to 6 at the home of Mrs. Hawkins, Twelfth Avenue and Boulevard. A fine program will be given, and a lovely surprise awaits the guests.

And the next week on September 16:

The Hawkins and Limbocker Tea was largely attended and about sixty ladies enjoyed the surprise, an automobile ride.

102

Then came the parade of automobiles:

> Mrs. George Hawkins' beautifully decorated car, trimmed in graceful clusters of the wisteria, intertwined with the glossy green of smilax, with her daughters, Cecile and Hazel dressed in white, made one of the most beautiful features of the parade and deservedly received first prize.

All newspaper entries confirm the fact that G. W. Hawkins represented the new industry in the Heights. He early established an automobile business in Houston and besides had an agency to sell automobile licenses throughout Harris County. The story is often told that Mr. Hawkins himself got the first license number each year until Governor Ferguson decided that he wanted License No. 1 for the Governor's car. What seems more likely is that during Governor Jim Ferguson's term of office the newly created State Highway Department registered cars under act of the legislature. Opposition to the act came from the local governments which had sought to retain the registration fees. Compromise was effected when the state returned a portion of the fees to the counties. This would indicate that Mr. Hawkins had been getting Harris County No. 1 license, which was no longer available, and that the governor got the first plate under the new law.

The "50 Years Ago" column of the *Houston Post,* on August 26, 1955 had this entry:

> Charles Caplen, 906 Tulane, the Preston Avenue bicycle dealer, has purchased an Oldsmobile touring runabout from Hawkins' Auto and Gas Engine Company.

This Mr. Caplen was one of the first residents of the Heights to have a telephone. He put his phone out on the front porch so that neighbors could use it while he was at work.

Mrs. Peacock was the first woman in the Heights (and the second in Houston) to drive a car. Her first automobile, however, was unsatisfactory; the wheel was too high. So she and Mr. Peacock went to Harrisburg to see the kind that the Milbys had bought. They liked it and decided to get the same make. So their second car was a Warren, very pretty with brass trimmings, mahogany woodwork, acetylene lights and all complete with license number 247. But like the first car, it cranked at the side.

THE BAYOU

In the early days of the Heights, people were conscious of living "out of town" and children loved the woods. White Oak Bayou circled the Heights on the south and west boundaries and "going to the bayou" was the favorite picnic for neighborhood groups. There were muscadine grapes and plenty of berries in season. In fact, the housewife could get buckets of grapes and berries from peddlers if the children did not go hunting for them.

The woods started a couple of blocks beyond Railroad (now Nicholson) and the tramp to the bayou was an easy walk and offered great fun to the children of the Heights. It also offered temptation to the boys when spring came and swimming holes were free pools. One particularly popular swimming hole was called "Folse's" at the Bayou on 8th Street. Others were known as "Rocky Bottom," "Loggy," and "Willow Bend."

As the vacant lots sold, and the houses built up, streets filled in the old wooded districts and children lost their feeling for picking violets and swinging on muscadine vines.

THE BALL PARK

On 19th, out past Railroad, on the south side of the street, near the woods, the famous Houston Heights Amusement Park was well fenced in. Stone and Webster had bought out the old street car company and new models of electric street cars brought crowds out to the best ball park around Houston. The only other big ball park then was Brunner, out in what is now called West End. Both parks drew big crowds.

CLUBS-
SOCIAL SERVICE
ORGANIZATIONS-
LODGES

HOUSTON HEIGHTS LITERARY CLUB

Since its first settlement a very decided civic activity had marked the Heights, the Houston Heights Literary Club being the outstanding organization for women. On January 15, 1900, sixteen women of the Heights met at the home of Mrs. C. R. Cummings and formed the Literary Club. Almost immediately after organization of the club, the president, Mrs. Cummings, moved from the Heights and Mrs. C. A. McKinney succeeded in office.

In the famous *Blue Book* for 1907-1908 is the following entry:

HOUSTON HEIGHTS LITERARY CLUB

Organized January, 1899. Membership 35. Meets every Wednesday from October to June at home of president. Officers and executive board: Mrs. W. G. Love, president; Mrs. W. W. Kellogg, first vice-president; Mrs. D. M. Duller, second vice-president; Mrs. Geo. C. Van Demark, recording secretary; Mrs. M. Sheehan, corresponding secretary; Mrs. P. B. Thornton, treasurer. Executive board; Mesdames W. G. Love, W. W. Kellogg, D. M. Duller, Geo. C. Van Demark, F. F. Dexter, W. E. Bennett, and H. N. Jones. Course of study for 1907-8, "American Studies."

Mrs. C. A. McKinney gave 1900 for the club's date of organization, so evidently the *Blue Book* made a mistake in its earlier date.

Meetings were held at the home of the president until increased membership made it necessary to have a club room. Mr. Carter then gave space in his power house at the waterworks on 19th Avenue.

HOUSTON HEIGHTS WOMAN'S CLUB

Meanwhile the Literary Club was outgrowing its single interest and expanding into enough departments to incorporate itself into the more general title of Woman's Club. In February, 1911, the Arts and Crafts Club, the Musical and Social Club, and the original Literary Club merged into the Houston Heights Woman's Club. All these different groups had come from the membership of the Literary Club or its associates. The charter members of the Woman's Club were: Mesdames W. E. Bennett, O. F. Carroll, Thomas S. Lowry, A. W. Cooley, G. W. Hawkins, S. H. Webber, W. A. Renn, C. A. McKinney, W. A. McNeill, M. D. Ritter, H. S. Robinson, A. B. Sheldon, P. B. Thornton, W. B. Welling.

Also in 1911, Mr. and Mrs. D. D. Cooley gave ground at 1846 Harvard for a club house and immediately plans were made for the building. *The Gilded Fool,* starring E. V. Whitty, was the first benefit sponsored by the ladies for the building fund. The club members also promoted a carnival at the playground for the same purpose. The *Suburbanite* has notice of the formal opening of the Club House on Friday, October 18, 1912.

The cost of the building was $1,500 and by way of comparison the price of the piano (financed by the Music Study Department) was the same amount. Under the able direction of Mrs. W. A. Renn, President of the Woman's Club, the members had their building clear of debt within a year of its erection. Their only trouble was the stage. It was built high, when ladies wore skirts that touched the floor, and twice had to be lowered as skirts got higher and higher.

EARLY CHARITY WORK OF THE CLUB WOMEN

Aside from its cultural character, the old Literary Club was an agency for great good among the poor in the Heights. The ladies held a ball once a year at the old skating rink and the proceeds were used as a charity fund. In various other ways the treasury of the club was replenished to serve as a community chest. Committees were appointed to investigate calls for aid and an amount of money was disbursed. The ladies would file the request together with a report on actual conditions found to warrant help, and then would give food and medical aid as far as they were able. There was no other social service available.

Later, the Woman's Club also fostered the first school library in the Heights. Actually in the beginning the books were kept in the principal's office, but the teachers could send there and secure material for classroom use. At least the club had provided books. Very few schools in those days had a library room provided to house the books.

UNITED CHARITIES

When the Literary Club in February, 1911, merged with its sub-divisions to form the Woman's Club, it must have made other arrangements for its charity work because the *Suburbanite* on March 11, 1911, shows members of the Literary Club forming a new organization for that specific purpose:

> At a meeting held at the home of Mrs. M. Sheehan Monday afternoon for the purpose of forming a United Charity Organization in the Heights, the following officers were elected: President, Rev. C. A. Earl; Vice-President, Mrs. J. M. Limbocker; Treasurer, Mrs. M. Sheehan; Recording Secretary, Mrs. E. F. Patterson; Corresponding Secretary, Mrs. W. A. Renn.

A few weeks later the *Suburbanite* gives an encouraging report on its tag day receipts for charity sponsored by this new organization. The following year the newspaper again mentioned Tag Day and named the ladies responsible during Christmas week ''to tag all going and coming on the street cars." Each lady had a number of young helpers appointed for different hours. These young ladies would board the car as it went round the belt and persuade each passenger to buy a tag.

Perhaps the dread disease that gripped all Houston was the immediate cause for the organization of the United Charities. On April 6, 1912, the *Suburbanite* gives notice about closed theaters and public places of meeting all over Houston and the Heights:

> Cerebo-Spinal Meningitis. What do you know about it? Let us urge you to learn more about it by coming to the Baptist Temple, Thursday . . .

The club women of the Heights founded their different groups for mutual pleasure and cultural improvement, but they also considered social work and educational help as part of their reason for organization.

SOCIAL SERVICE LEADERS

Mention should be made here of outstanding business women in the Heights, each of whom achieved distinction in her professional life of social service.

First place belongs to Mrs. Hortense Ward, who with her husband, Judge W. H. Ward, founded the law firm of Ward and Ward. Mrs. Ward had, in 1910, made news when she was the first woman in Texas to pass the bar examination. But her great contribution to the women of her state lay in her successful battle for "Property Rights for Women."

On March 21, 1913, Governor Colquitt signed the bill defining separate and community property of the husband and the wife and removing disabilities of married women in the management and control of their separate property. The governor then gave his pen to Mrs. Ward. The civil status of women in Texas gained recognition because of Mrs. Ward's intelligent and competent efforts in connection with marital property rights for women of the state. At the time the bill was signed in Texas there were only two remaining states in the Union where women were denied the right to handle their own property and personal earnings.

Mrs. Ward's mother, Mrs. Louisa Sparks, a widow with a large family, for years lived on West 16th and was prominent in the north end of the Heights. Mrs. Ward's sister, Miss Ella Sparks, married Charlie Udell, and lived on West 18th. Mrs. Ward's only surviving daughter in 1955 is Mrs. John H. Crooker, Sr.

Another outstanding professional woman in the Heights was Miss Ferdie Trichel, who lived with her family on West 17th. Miss Trichel organized and helped to build the Newsboys Home in Houston, which around 1912 was a haven for teen-agers needing protection.

Today the average newsboy is the youngster saving for college or for some extra hobby of his own. But when Miss Trichel was interested, the ordinary boy selling newspapers needed necessities, and in many instances needed most of all a home and good social environment. Miss Trichel tried to provide that. She was a plain spoken, remarkably quiet little woman, whose soft voice went a long way in winning help for her boys.

CHORAL CLUB

Fred F. Dexter started a choral club about 1909, and over his store, on 17th and Rutland, he held practice. People joined not because they could sing but because Mr. Dexter made the lessons enjoyable. At the time he was the assistant musical director and accompanist for the Houston Quartette Society, and he and Mrs. Dexter gave themselves freely to the encouragement of musical organization in the Heights.

PROGRAMS AND TALLIES

After the gay nineties, the early 1900's were much the same. Formality with frills was the order of the day. Young ladies brought home tallies when they played "high five" and programs when they attended dances. These trophies were pinned in great clusters on the bedroom wall.

Also young ladies wore many frills and enjoyed dressing up. Then it was that the Neaubeaux Club was organized by Misses Abbie Mae Hartley, Blanche Bennett, and Lucille Inkley. This organization was strictly for young ladies with their escorts, the name notwithstanding. And it was an important club in the Heights after 1909 or 1910. The *Suburbanite* records all the "delightful" parties of the Neaubeaux Club.

Its membership included the group out of high school. In 1955, one of its early members said that many of the original members still meet, that when an old girl comes back to visit or to live, she simply takes up where she left off.

No record of charter members could be found, but the *Suburbanite* files tell of parties held in December of 1911 at the home of Misses Bessie Boyle, Dorothy Hamm, and Althea Lane, and lists members who were present: Marabel Hamilton, Marie Malsch, Helen Whitfield, Marcella Jones, Elsie Vieweger, Marguerite Malsch, Helen McNeill, Garnett Robinson, Ida Bell, Beulah Barber, Bessie Boyle, Abbie Mae Hartley, Lucille Inkley, Janette Eller, Blanche Bennett, Dorothy Hamm, Mollie Mae Thornton, Edith Yantis, Maud Yantis, Ruby Webb, Mrs. G. J. Robinson.

THE SOUTH END EMBROIDERY CLUB

About the same time as the organization of the Neaubeaux, a group of ladies, chiefly from the neighborhood of Coombs Terrace, organized a social club that for many years enjoyed its weekly sewing circle and luncheon in the home of its different members. The club did not specify any civic reason for its being, but its members were leading women in the early development of the Heights and their embroidery club lasted for years. The following names were given by the daughter of one of the first members: Mesdames E. A. Taylor, Harry Van Demark, D. D. Smeaton, J. M. Limbocker, D. Barker, W. P. Hamblen, Hiram Gilliam, H. S. Robinson, P. M. Granberry, S. H. Webber, J. S. Purdy, W. C. Purdy, Julia Coombs, Julia Hamilton, Chas. King, and Frank Witte.

110

THE SUNSHINE SOCIETY

The Houston Heights Sunshine Society was organized in March, 1910, by Mrs. J. A. Gillette with the following ladies as charter members: Mesdames P. O. Endt, S. D. Wilkins, E. M. Johnston, C. Schleeter, T. A. Sinclair, P. B. Thornton, R. J. Shallcross, J. W. Blake, Maud Ketterman. Others who soon joined were: Mesdames E. F. Patterson, C. B. Udell, C. R. Allman, Louisa Sparks, W. Turney, M. Sheehan, J. M. Grant, John Dunlop, H. K. Hodes, H. Yoakum, O. C. Miller, A. Como, S. A. Bozell, R. D. Jeter, Eugene Cook, R. J. Webb, F. C. Van Liew, C. A. McKinney, Belle M. Costello, J. W. Scott.

Mrs. Costello was for years the society editor of the *Houston Chronicle* and once a week in that paper she had a column devoted to the interest of the Sunshine Society.

The organization's chief end was to make life more pleasant for the old. The ladies kept a list of "four-score" residents whose birthdays they always remembered. In 1914, Grandma Burns was outstanding with her party given at the home of Mrs. Shallcross on Mrs. Burns' 108th birthday. The members made annual visits to bring cheer to the old ladies living at Sheltering Arms. They maintained wheel chairs for those in need, made layette outfits, and in one instance financed a blind girl's musical education. On April 27, 1912, at Mrs. Udell's home the Society had a silver tea "for Miss Elmo Randall, blind pianist who will graduate next month." For many years the Heights Sunshine Society carried on in neighborhood fashion what the Community Chest later did through organized charity. There was a difference, however, in that the Sunshine Society did not consider its work *charity,* and most of its cases were not in need of anything except the remembrance.

TUESDAY SOCIAL CLUB

At the home of Mrs. John Dunlop in May, 1915, the Tuesday Social Club organized with its first five members: Mesdames T. A. Sinclair, Walter Davis, R. J. Shallcross, R. E. Patterson, and John Dunlop. Specifically social in its purpose this club limits its membership to twelve. Mrs. Dunlop in 1955 tells that after forty years some of the original members still belong and still attend the social functions planned for its closely associated group.

INDEPENDENT ORDER OF ODDFELLOWS

Houston Heights Lodge No. 225, Independent Order of Oddfellows was issued a charter on May 6, 1905, by F. H. Kneeland. The petitioners for the charter were: G. W. Hawkins, R. H. Towles, P. V. Myers, R. E. Turrentine, and J. S. Patterson. The first report, December 31, 1905, showed the following 43 members: G. W. Arnold, A. A. Berger, J. R. Brown, W. O. Backus, Sylvester Branham, W. V. Cox, J. C. Denny, T. E. Dillworth, F. B. Davis, J. W. Foote, B. G. Fenner, J. A. Gillette, G. W. Hawkins, H. E. Henrichsen, Charles Horn, R. A. Hudgins, W. H. Hergist, L. H. Hood, F. M. Johnson, R. D. Jeter, W. G. Love, J. B. Lucas, G. T. Lowery, P. V. Myers, C. A. McPherson, J. S. Patterson, L. A. Pledger, H. M. Platt, M. W. Parry, B. Patella, Ben Reinicke, H. H. Reeves, J. C. Smith, R. H. Towles, W. L. Thompson, R. E. Turrentine, W. B. Vaughn, F. C. Van Liew, G. W. Wilson, C. A. Wallace, Charles Winkler, J. H. Wilson, J. R. Gadon.

The story of Fraternal Hall has already outlined the earliest attempt of the Oddfellows to build a place for their work in the Heights. When Fraternal Hall burned in 1912, the lodge had to start anew. Seven faithful members during this period kept the organization alive and met in the hall above Dexter's store on 17th and Rutland. In later years the Oddfellows would grow into a strong group able to build another home of which today the lodge is justly proud.

REBEKAH LODGE

The Cleopatra Rebekah Lodge No. 62 was organized in February, 1906, by the following charter members: P. V. Myers, G. W. Hawkins, J. S. Patterson, T. A. Goldnap, and William Broker, and Mesdames Elizabeth Brown, Nettie Hawkins, Clara Patterson, Lulu Wallace, and Dora Harris.

All of these members had withdrawn from Esther Rebekah Lodge No. 6. Fifteen more members came in by initiation, making a total of 25 members. The first meetings were held in the Wallace-Johnson Hall over the store that later became known as the Nineteenth Avenue Drug Store. After organization, the lodge moved to Fraternal Hall where it lost all records when the hall burned in 1912.

Next the members met in Dexter's Hall and changed their name to Houston Heights Rebekah Lodge No. 62. Under that title they would build their own hall and grow into a strong unit of their organization.

HEIGHTS MASONIC LODGE

The John H. Reagan Lodge No. 1037 was chartered December 12, 1910. It was organized over the volunteer fire department building, next to Dr. William Olive's Drug Store at 910 Yale Street. The charter members were:

Backus, W. O.	Horn, Chas., Jr.
Bernard, A. C.	Horn, Chas., Sr.
Coulter, A. M.	Johnston, E. M.
Damron, P. E.	Neville, E. F.
Dietrich, Emil G.	Olive, Wm.
Fowler, J. C.	Ratzel, R.
French, J. M.	Reimers, H. G.
Gordon, J. A.	Shallcross, R. J.
Groves, A. E.	Stiel, J. C.
Hart, C. C.	Turnsek, O. J.
Helms, Jas. F.	Ward, W. H.

Only two of these first members are now living: A. C. Bernard and R. J. Shallcross.

The Masters of Reagan Lodge from its beginning until annexation were: J. M. French, Jas. F. Helms, W. H. Ward, A. C. Bernard, C. C. Hart, Sr., R. J. Shallcross, C. I. Voss, J. A. Jackson, and R. D. Hardcastle.

BIOGRAPHY

FOUNDERS

OSCAR MARTIN CARTER

Oscar Martin Carter's c o m p l e t e life story should be written because it is stranger than fiction and needs a thick book to do justice to its merits. O. M. Carter was a genius and for that reason went through life a rather lonely victim of his own great talents that set him off from the ordinary man.

He was born September 2, 1842, at Salem, Massachusetts. Left an orphan when very young, he was bound out to people who were cruel to him. He ran away, and at Northfield, Vermont, he learned the tinner's trade. Later he joined a pack train hauling freight across western plains. In this way he first saw Colorado and became interested in mining.

Carter's versatility in business m a n a g e m e n t and in professional skills baffles belief. He worked as a cook for an ox-team caravan; at Central City he mined; all through the Mid-West he plied his trade as a tinner; he worked for the Union Pacific Railroad at Omaha; at Ashland, Nebraska he operated a hardware store, a tin shop, and a flour mill, all at the same time that he managed Governor Saunders' race for the U. S. Senate.

For six years he was the government's trader with the Sioux Indians at the Rosebud Indian Agency. After 1885, he became president of six banks c e n t e r i n g around Omaha, while he was also president of the American Loan and Trust

115

Company in Omaha. In 1887, Carter sold his interests in Nebraska and came to Houston. By 1890, he had bought both the Houston City Street Railway C o m p a n y and the Bayou City Street Railway Company in the interests of his Omaha and South Texas Land Company venture.

Mr. Carter was the inventor of the Carter Bit, and he manufactured the Standard Collapsible Rotary Drill and Core Barrel. He operated a gold and silver mine in Colorado. The record of his achievements is fantastic. And the greatest of his a c c o m p l i s h m e n t s was his real estate venture in Houston Heights.

On April 25, 1866, at Plattsmouth, Nebraska, he was married to Miss Cinderella Thomas. There were six children born to this marriage. But for years in Houston, Mr. Carter never made a home, living at the Hutchins House or his hotel.

In 1915, his first wife died at her home in Denver. In 1920, Mr. Carter married Miss Nellie Green. From that time until his death on January 6, 1928, he made his home at 1316 Heights Boulevard.

Many people remember that Mr. Carter could have taken their homes and he r e f u s e d to do so. The c i t i z e n s of Houston Heights in their d e a l i n g s with Mr. Carter found always complete honesty and gentle courtesy. This history in its probings uncovered no record of any suit involving a charge of unfair treatment in the vast real estate deals that Mr. Carter handled in developing Houston Heights. Mr. Carter in more ways than one was truly the Founder of the Heights.

DANIEL DENTON COOLEY

Born in Binghamton, New York, in 1850, Daniel Denton Cooley was the d e s c e n d a n t of early English settlers of Massachusetts. He grew up in his native place and attended school and business college in Binghamton.

As a young man he went West and settled at Ashland, Nebraska. Here he engaged in the mercantile business and became cashier in the First National Bank of which O. M.

Carter was president. In 1887, he became associated as treasurer and general manager with Carter's newly organized Omaha and South Texas Land Company.

By 1892, the company's vast real estate venture had become a reality and "lots in an improved addition" were for sale. Mr. Cooley's office after 1893 was in the west corner of the hotel built by the company on 19th and Ashland. Ilis home at 1802 Boulevard was the first erected on that street.

From the beginning of the Heights development, Mr. Cooley had worked to establish schools, and in 1894 Cooley School opened. For years Mr. Cooley served on the school board for the Heights.

In 1882, D. D. Cooley married Miss Helen Grace Winfield; and when the couple located in the Heights, they brought with them their three small sons. The family was active in the first Episcopal services at St. Stephen's Mission, held for a number of years at Cooley School. Later the Cooleys were leaders in establishing St. Andrew's Episcopal Church on West 20th.

Mr. Cooley's interests were varied. He engaged in the real estate business, was identified with the South Texas National Bank, and with H. F. MacGregor in the operation of the Electric Street Railway Company. About 1903, he became a member of the insurance firm of Childress and Taylor, which was later renamed Cooley, Schweikart and Seaman. He continued as head of this firm until his death in 1933.

Mr. Cooley and his family were all unusually affable and inclined to join in all social and civic functions of their community. For that reason Old Houston Heights felt very close to the tall, white-haired gentleman, who to many people represented the "Father of Houston Heights."

CHARLES A. MCKINNEY

Charles A. McKinney was born in 1855. While yet a young man, he located in Princeton, Illinois, where he became secretary of the Illinois Masonic Insurance Company. He also served as superintendent of the Sunday School of the Princeton Methodist Church.

In 1878, he was married in Princeton to Miss Kate Bacon of that city. In 1885, the McKinneys moved to Omaha, where Mr. McKinney assumed a position with the American Loan and Trust Company of Omaha, of which O. M. Carter was president.

Two years later Mr. Carter went to Texas in connection with his proposed Omaha and South Texas Land Company, and there he bought all street car facilities in Houston. After Carter started street car lines to the Heights in 1892, Mr. and Mrs. McKinney and Mrs. McKinney's widowed mother, Mrs. Cynthia A. Bacon, moved to Houston. Mr. McKinney was made Secretary and Treasurer of the Houston City Street Railway Company and the Bayou City Street Railway Company.

In 1895, after Carter's dream of Houston Heights had materialized, the transit system was sold. Mr. McKinney then resumed his banking career. He became associated with the South Texas Commercial National Bank and remained with that institution until his death in 1922. For years he acted as Assistant Cashier.

In 1893, Mr. and Mrs. McKinney moved into their home at 1630 Heights Boulevard, making it their permanent residence. Besides Mrs. McKinney's mother, who lived with them, Miss Ella McKinney, Mr. McKinney's sister, was often a member of the household. She died at the McKinney home in 1934.

Mr. and Mrs. McKinney loved children and since they had none of their own, throughout their married life they extended help to families who needed assistance for their children. Mr. McKinney acted as superintendent for a number of churches, and for years delighted in teaching Sunday School at the Presbyterian Church. His first interest was always directed toward helping youth. In his will he left the bulk of his estate to Faith Home. Mrs. McKinney died in 1943 and her will made the same provision.

JOHN A. MILROY

John A. Milroy was born in 1862, of Scotch lineage, on a farm near the village of York, New York. He grew up there and attended school and college in his native section of New York State. In 1889, he married Miss Nellie Jane Hamilton, of the Neighboring village of Caledonia, New York; and in the same year he took his bride to Seattle, Washington, where he engaged in the real estate business.

In 1893, Mr. Milroy arrived in Houston where he became associated with O. M. Carter, founder and owner of Houston Heights, which was at that time in its initial state of development.

By 1894, Mr. Milroy had sent for his family and established a home at 16th and Harvard. Here they remained until 1898 when they moved to the house at 1102 Boulevard, since known as the Milroy home. Mr. and Mrs. Milroy had three children: Helen Douglas, Margaret Adair, and William Hamilton.

Of the early group associated with Mr. Carter in founding the Heights, only Mr. Milroy stayed on through the years. When all the other business developments of the original Omaha and South Texas Land Company had simmered down to the simple proposition of selling real estate, then only a real estate expert was needed. In that capacity John A. Milroy guided the "Houston Heights Office" for almost 25 years. Only in 1917 did he sever, with deep regret, his connection with O. M. Carter, when he left the Heights Office to open up his own real estate business.

As manager of the Heights Office, Mr. Milroy had learned to know the community interests of the Heights and this knowledge served him in his long public career. At the first council meeting of the Municipality, we find Mr. Milroy as an alderman, then as secretary of the council, and later as member of the school board. In 1899, he was elected Mayor of the Heights and was seven times re-elected. Finally after serving eight years he asked to withdraw.

On April 17, 1907, the *Houston Chronicle* ran a lengthy story of a testimonial assembly at Fraternal Hall when the people of Houston Heights paid homage to Mr. Milroy and presented him with a beautiful chest of silver. Judge W. G. Love in his testimonial speech said: "Your official conduct has been characterized by that patience and diplomacy which small men do not possess." Judge Love spoke for the people of Houston Heights.

On August 19, 1918, at the comparatively early age of fifty-six, John Milroy died. The Heights lost a good man.

MAYORS

MAYOR LOVE

William Graston Love was born in Dallas County, Texas, on January 17, 1869, the son of William E. and Hulda Graston Love. In 1877, the family moved to Salado, Texas where the father engaged in farming and merchandising.

W. G. Love received his education in the common schools and Salado College. Later he attended the University of Texas and was graduated in 1889 with the degree of LL. B. That same year he was admitted to the bar of Texas and began his legal practice at Luling, where he remained until 1893 when he moved to Houston. The *City Directory* lists him as residing in 1894 on the Heights Boulevard between 14th and 15th.

In 1896, he became the first mayor when the Heights voted to incorporate as a municipality. He served three one-year terms and then became President of the Houston Heights School Board. Moreover, Mr. Love served his community as legal advisor and perhaps aided most in this capacity because the Heights was still a giant real estate proposition just emerging into a settled social order.

In 1907, Mr. Love was appointed District Attorney to fill an unexpired term for the criminal district comprising Harris and Galveston Counties. In 1908, he was elected for a two-year term to the same office. In 1910, he retired to attend to his private practice.

He was married in 1901 to his second wife, Miss Lillie Webb, daughter of Dr. W. T. Webb, well known physician and member of an old family of Mobile, Alabama, who had come to Flatonia, Texas in 1874. They had one son, William Hamilton Love.

In appearance Judge Love looked not unlike Abraham Lincoln, tall, determined, and because of this likeness seemingly typical of the pioneer lawyer. He was dignified in bearing, but (also like Lincoln) jovial and warm in his associations. His last home in the Heights, at 15th and Boulevard, was noted for its hospitality and its genuine spirit of friendly cheer. Mr. Love died June 30, 1926, aged 57 years.

MAYOR BARKER

David Barker was born in Bond County, Illinois, about ten miles from Greenville. He was the fourth of five children born to David and Malinda Stever Barker and he grew up on his parents' farm. His early life was rich in the security of a good home but poor in the opportunities for an education.

After a sunstroke young David Barker found himself unable for the hard work of the farm and untrained for scholastic enterprise. After several trials at night school and state employment, he finally bought a grocery store in a small town in Illinois called Old Ripley. He succeeded and bought other stores in neighboring settlements. He worked hard and studied harder.

In 1897, in Old Ripley, he married Miss Pauline Rilling. Shortly after their marriage, the young couple sold their stores and settled in Greenville. On an excursion trip to Texas, Mr. Barker discovered that he liked the country and instinctively felt that Texas also offered sound economic security.

121

He brought his wife to Texas in 1903 and settled in the Heights where his son and daughter were born. His shrewd self-education, his instinctive honesty, his warm kindliness of manner, and his quiet dignity all combined to make Mr. Barker an outstanding man. In Texas he entered the real estate business and his clients grew to trust his sharp appraisals and his honest figures.

In 1906, he was, at the insistance of his associates, forced into the nomination for mayor of the Heights. He served from April, 1907 to April, 1913. During that period, the Heights voted heavy bonds for improvements and Mr. Barker was chiefly responsible for the wise expenditure of this money and for the period of progress that marked his term of office.

After 1913, Mr. Barker served the City of Houston for years in various positions of trust. It would be impossible in this short sketch to enumerate his contributions, but this much should be said, that the Heights' only living ex-mayor for over fifty years has served his community with honor, dignity, and wisdom.

MAYOR ISBELL

Robert F. Isbell was born January 1, 1877, in Isbell, Alabama. He grew up in a large family of five brothers and four sisters. When he was about eighteen years of age, his parents moved to Nashville, and most of their children later settled near them in that city.

Robert Isbell became assistant manager of the Western Union in Nashville and married Miss Ruby Neville, daughter of Dr. E. F. Neville. After the birth of their son, the young couple moved to Houston in 1903 and built the Isbell homestead at 629 Heights Boulevard. For sixteen years Mr. Isbell was outstanding in the business circles of Houston and Southeast Texas. He organized the South Texas Oilmen's Association, was an early member of the Houston Club, belonged to the Lumbermen's Club, the Elks and other business and social groups.

Only once did he venture into politics, when in 1913 he ran for office of mayor of Houston Heights and won the election. At the time, Mr. Isbell was Secretary and Treasurer of the Fidelity Cotton Oil and Fertilizer Company. He was young when elected mayor and naturally still rising in his business career. When he was offered the position of manager of the Taft Industries, he could ill afford to stay in Houston. He resigned in August, 1914, as mayor and took his family to Taft, Texas. Later, still with Taft interests, Mr. Isbell moved to Portland, Texas, in the center of the Taft cotton production. Here, on February 19, 1920, Robert Isbell was accidentally shot. His passing was mourned by all who had known him. Few men of his age had made more lasting impression upon business associates, quite apart from hosts of personal friends, for warm, sturdy, intelligent leadership.

Mrs. Isbell and her son moved back to the old home on the Boulevard, where she still resides. The son, after receiving his Ph. D. from the University of Wisconsin, taught science and then was called to serve the U. S. Air Forces in the chemical warfare department. Today he is Colonel R. N. Isbell.

MAYOR MARMION

James Barrus Marmion was born to Henry M. and Mary Elizabeth Marmion on April 25, 1871, in Washington Parish, Louisiana. When he was still small, his family moved to Houston; and when he was fifteen, his father was permanently injured. James, as the eldest son, with four brothers and two sisters to help care for, went to work selling papers and acting as messenger boy for the Ben Reisner Company.

Four years later, he owned his own blacksmith and carriage shop and had four men working for him. This energy and determination characterized J. B. Marmion throughout life. Possibly, too, because he had to push a boy's strength to meet a man's responsibility, he became adept and practiced in aggressive struggle.

The Marmion family had lived in old Fifth Ward. There J. B. Marmion settled after his marriage in November, 1893 to Miss Mary Josephine Harris. In 1910, he took his growing family to Houston Heights, where immediately he became a leader in civic affairs.

In August, 1914, R. F. Isbell, Mayor of Houston Heights, resigned from office and the group who had supported Isbell put up W. P. Hamblen, Jr., for the special election called for September 5 to fill the vacancy. J. B. Marmion, nominated on a ticket which identified him as opposed to corporate interests, defeated Hamblen. Marmion was later re-elected and was still in office when the Heights was annexed in February, 1918.

After that event, Mr. Marmion served in various positions at City Hall in Houston. His s c r a p b o o k unconsciously shows his personal preference in his different posts. For some time he was Park C o m m i s s i o n e r and most of his pictures were taken at Sam Houston Park (old City Park), of the grandstand, with his children in different beauty spots. In Marmion's report in 1915, while he was still Mayor of the Heights, he had pleaded for a park where children could play, s o m e t h i n g bigger and better than the old Heights Playground.

J. B. Marmion seems to have been the greatest fighter of our early Heights political leaders; but like most fighters, he was at heart a very gentle man, a man who loved his own children and who fought for parks for other people's children.

IN CONCLUSION

It is with pride that the people of the Heights can point to the early settlement of their community. This history has attempted to present facts, not deliberately sought as *good* but essentially evaluated as such, in evidence of the general character of early life in the Heights. However, because that life was more or less simple would not necessarily mean that it was a good life. What seems good sometimes may seem so only because our vision is partial. But in this chronicle as the pieces were put together to complete the whole, the picture that resulted seemed fundamentally sound and the pride seemed fully justifiable.

BIBLIOGRAPHY

City Directories for the years 1890-1918.

City of Houston and Harris County, Texas; World's Columbian Exposition Souvenir, Houston, Cumming and Sons, 1893.

Council of Houston Heights, Minutes. 1896-1903, 1911-1918.

Green, Chas. D. *Fire Fighter of Houston, 1838-1915.* Houston, 1915.

Handbook of Texas, 2 vols. Austin, Texas State Historical Association, 1952.

Houston, a History and Guide. Houston, Anson Jones Press, 1942.

Houston Illustrated, a Few Facts ... pub. by *Houston Daily Herald,* 1893.

Industrial Advantages of Houston, Texas and Environs. Houston, 1894.

Key to the City of Houston. Houston, 1908.

Records. Office of County Clerk, Harris County.

Scrapbook at Heights Library.

Standard Blue Book of Texas; Edition de luxe of Houston. Who's Who, *1907-8.*

The Suburbanite, Heights Newspaper, Jan., 1905-Feb., 1920.

Telephone Directories.

FOR BIOGRAPHY

Davis and Grobe, editors. *New Encyclopedia of Texas,* 2 vols. n.d.

Johnson, Frank W. *A History of Texas and Texans,* 5 vols., 1914.

Wharton, Clarence. *Texas under Many Flags.* 5 vols., 1930.

INDEX

A

Adams, Marjorie Lappine, 91
All Saints Catholic Church, 64-65, 74
Allen, A. C., 16, 17
Allen, J. K., 16, 17
Allen, Lester L., 66
Allman, C. R., 111
Ammons, Rev. Evander, 65
Ammons, Mrs. E., 88
Andrews, M. L. O., 43
Annexation, 43
Arnold, G. W., 112
Austin, John, 16
Austin, William T., 16
Automobile, The early, 102-103

B

Backus, W. O., 31, 112, 113
Bacon, Mrs. Cynthia A., 86
Bagby, C. Ethel, 58
Baker, Nelson A., 26, 35, 79
Bakery, 35
Ball Park, or Houston Heights Amusement Park, 104
Baptist Church, First, 63-64, 75
Baptist Temple, 33, 65, 75
Barber, Beulah, 110
Barker, D., 22, 35, 41, 83, 99, 121-122
Barker, Mrs. D., 110
Barnes, Big Boy, 85
Barziza, Mrs. Florence, 88
Bayou, The, 104
Beavens, Mrs. C. C., 88
Beavens, Emily, 88
Bell, Ida, 56, 110
Bender, Mrs. J. M., 88
Bennett, Blanche, 56, 88, 110
Bennett, Mrs. W. E., 105, 106
Berger, A. A., 112
Bernard, A. C., 113
Blackburn, Catherine Cox, 91
Blake, Mrs. J. W., 111

Borgstrom, Sophia, 56, 86
Boyle, Bessie, 110
Boyle, John T., 27, 35, 43
Bozell, Mrs. S. A., 111
Bradshaw Feed Company, 102
Bradshaw, W. D., 99
Branham, Sylvester, 112
Brashear, F. G., 30
Brashear, I. W., 17
Brashear, Mrs. Sarah, 17
Brashear's John Austin Grant, 16-17
Bridges, 23
Brock, I. V., 59
Broker, William, 112
Brooke, H. D., 38
Brown, Mrs. Elizabeth, 112
Brown, J. R., 112
Browning, Hattie Stone, 91
Burge, Marian, 87
Burlingame, Evelyn, 56
Burlingame, Lottie, 58
Butler, Lee, 48
Byrd, Sigman, 18

C

Camp Tom Ball, 97-98
Caplen, Charles, 103
Carpenter, Mrs. J. C., 55
Carter, Christine Freeman, 91
Carter, O. M., 15, 17, 18, 19, 20, 21, 25, 26, 27, 28, 31, 34, 37, 38, 50, 61, 65, 79, 95, 100, 106, 115-116
Charity Work, 107
Christian, Rose, 56
Clark, Lucy, 53
Clarke, F. E., 16
Cloud, Dr. R. E., 51
Colley, H. C., 43
Colley, Mrs. H. C., 57
Collins Memorial Church, 63, 73
Collins, Rev. M. D., 63
Colored Schools, 61
Como, Mrs. A., 111
Compo-board, 28-29

127